D

Sorry its late!

Hope you enjoy this

Love from Matt & Emma.

PAPER
BLISS
350
CASTELLO DI MUSSOMELI
ITALIA
350
CASTELLO DI MUSSOMELI
ITALIA

Illustrations, decorative papers,
photos (and this font!)
all by Skye Rogers.

PAPER BLISS

Projects and musings on life in the paper lane

Skye Rogers

HarperCollinsPublishers
harpercollins.com.au

any money is deposited or withdrawn.
Amount of
Credit Balance
abcdefghij

Badger's boyhood bear,
mid-late 1960s

For Badger, my paper tiger.
Thank you for your support,
enthusiasm, love and general
pleating and folding abilities!
And thanks also to the two
little lads, Sam and Tom,
for their well-crafty ways.

Contents

Introduction

I have been an illustrator for a good part of my adult life. My apprenticeship for this career was my childhood passion for drawing on, cutting up and stamping on bits of paper then pasting them together. If there was a piece of paper handy, then there was my object of entertainment — it could be endlessly applied to make so many things. Once drawn upon or otherwise decorated, my little piece of paper could be fashioned into an aeroplane to be sent across the classroom, become a little paper house with cut-out windows, or a dress for a doll in need of a special outfit. For something so humble, that piece of paper sure had some uses.

The best thing about paper was its availability and the fact that it wasn't something my mother had to buy especially for me — it was always lying around. This is something I still love about making things with paper: it's still always there, it's recyclable, and can be fashioned into any number of wonderful, whimsical, sturdy or beautiful things with a little bit of thought and care.

I don't know that this early desire to make things ever quite leaves us. It's the sort of joy that still feels so pure, even though it can be hard, at times, to justify. I spent a whole summer not so long ago sitting around my lounge room cutting, pasting, drawing and sewing like a

abcdefghijkl
butterfly

woman possessed. Some of the looks I received from visitors were on the astonished side — this wasn't productive, this wasn't what a grown woman should be doing, this wasn't making money.

But from this fever of creativity came my burgeoning little business, Skye's The Limit ('what is life but a series of inspired follies?' asked George Bernard Shaw). I loved the idea of creating accessible, interesting, affordable art — and with my love of all things paper, along with an awareness of the huge popularity that stationery goods currently enjoy — greeting cards were the obvious canvas for me to take my experiments a step further. In late 2007, I began merrily printing my designs onto lovely quality card from my desktop printer. I was in heaven!

My non-income period proved fruitful, and my work was well received. The business has since grown to become something that has had to move out of the office, the front room, and the lounge room. And although I love running my business — it is so much a part of me — my greatest joy is still playing with bits of paper, and coming up with new ways to use time-old ideas.

Along the way I have often been asked 'How did you come up with that?' and I realised that there are so many people out there wanting a few tips on bringing some ideas together from the simplest materials. Being something of a bowerbird, I thought gathering some projects that I have considered, admired or completed over the years would be a great idea. I love sharing these ideas and so have developed the projects in this book to help and inspire others in their creative journey. *Folly hunters unite!*

Further to that, I also want this book to be an inspiration for both big kids and small. I hope it will encourage the 'big kids' to think about their own creativity, to challenge and question themselves: Can I do what a primary school kid can do? Can I 'let go' enough? Can I remember what the joy of creating feels like? Almost everyone has some memory of creating something that was praised (or, sadly, derided), when they were young. Often coming back to that space can be scary. This book will, I hope, help show the way back to that early pleasure we took in our creative attempts.

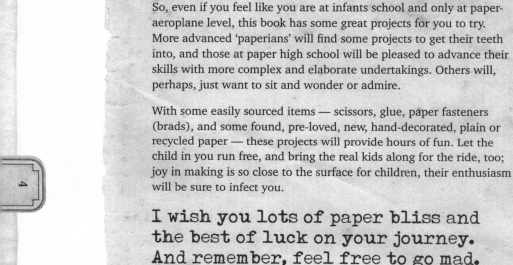

I have watched, often in awe, as people connect with that long forgotten person. It is a beautiful thing to see develop.

So, even if you feel like you are at infants school and only at paper-aeroplane level, this book has some great projects for you to try. More advanced 'paperians' will find some projects to get their teeth into, and those at paper high school will be pleased to advance their skills with more complex and elaborate undertakings. Others will, perhaps, just want to sit and wonder or admire.

With some easily sourced items — scissors, glue, paper fasteners (brads), and some found, pre-loved, new, hand-decorated, plain or recycled paper — these projects will provide hours of fun. Let the child in you run free, and bring the real kids along for the ride, too; joy in making is so close to the surface for children, their enthusiasm will be sure to infect you.

I wish you lots of paper bliss and the best of luck on your journey. And remember, feel free to go mad. It can sometimes be the mother of surprising inventions.

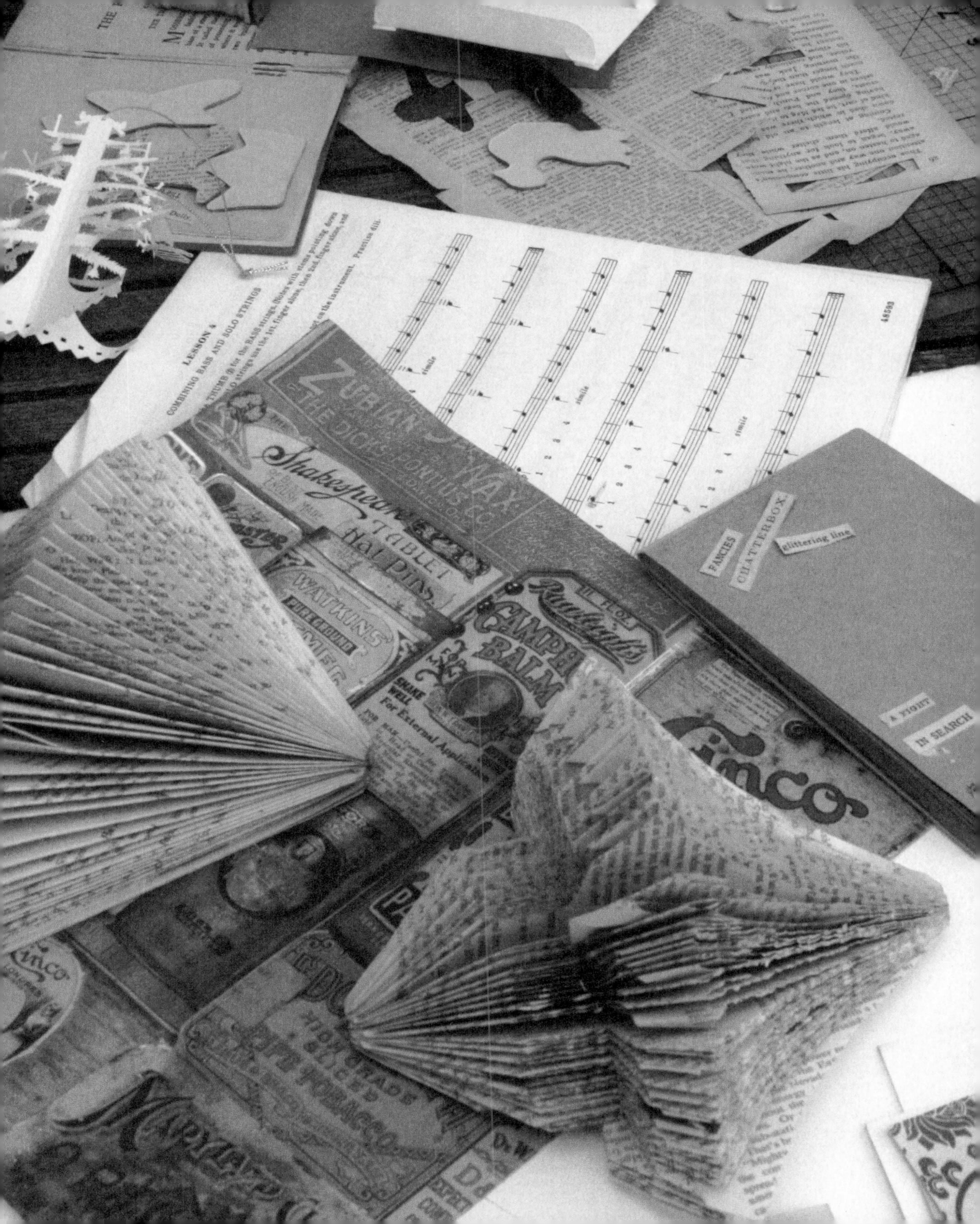
LESSON 4
COMBINING BASS AND SOLO STRINGS
simile
TABLET
WATKINS
PURE GROUND
SHAKE WELL
FANCIES
CHATTERBOX
glittering line
A FIGHT
IN SEARCH

Recycling

The amount of 'waste' that is tossed out in our affluent society is a boon for those of us who love to create imaginative objects from found bits and pieces. If you are anything like me, nothing is more satisfying than discovering in a pile of 'rubbish' awaiting the council pick-up a beautiful piece of wood, jars, vases, old tools and, sometimes, even paper. These days there is so much that can be found that to embark on a creative project will cost you next to nothing. And even more satisfying is that you are not only recycling and saving our landfill from overflowing you are actually upcycling. That is, you are not simply reusing a thrown away object but you are transforming it into something of value and beauty.

So keep upcycling to not only satisfy the creative spirit within, but to help our Earth, in some small way, to stay healthy.

25C NEDERLAND
25C NEDERLAND
malaysia
Canada 78
CANADA
éIRE €1
éIRE €1
éIRE €1
UNION OF MYANMAR
RSA
PILGRIM'S REST
20c
RSA
PILGRIM'S REST
20c
Performing Arts
ESPA
CORREOS
HONG KONG
MYANMAR HARP
K30
UNION OF MYANMAR
Australia
5c
2s
AUSTRALIA
REPUBLIK OSTERREICH
NEDERLAND €0,81
€0,65

It is better to create
than to be learned,
creating is the true essence of life.

BARTHOLD GEORG NIEBUHR

Toolkit

When embarking on making and creating, you don't want to be constantly searching for suitable tools, so before you start on anything put together a toolkit.

Your Basic Toolkit

UTILITY KNIFE/SCALPEL
I use a variety: a proper surgeon's scalpel with a 10a blade, and a smallish utility knife with a retractable blade available from newsagents or art-supply stores. The scalpel is the most precise, but it can be a bit scary. Store them safely by embedding the blade in a chunky eraser.

Using a utility knife and cutting mat is best kept for adults only.

CUTTING MAT
Called 'self-healing' these days. Nice to know!

SCISSORS
Both small and ordinary sized. Young kids are best watched carefully with sharp scissors.

SINGLE-HOLE PUNCH

DECORATIVE CRAFT PUNCHES
Available from art/craft stores.

STRING
I like plain, thin, creamy cotton string which you can buy in a large roll.

BRADS/PAPER FASTENERS
They come in all sizes and styles these days, but I prefer the plain shaped and black, white, silver or gold ones.

TRACING PAPER

PENCILS
Lead 3B and ordinary HB, and coloured pencils.

BRAYER OR ROLLING PIN
I use this to flatten, smooth and adhere bits of artwork together. Brayers are usually used in printmaking processes. They come in different sizes and have a cylindrical roller often made of rubber, and a handle. Mine is about 10cm wide. Rolling it gently but firmly over the surface of your pieces will reward you with a lovely even look and an artwork that will 'stay put'.

METAL RULER AND SET SQUARE

PVA GLUE/WHITE GLUE
So good for everything. PVA does most of everything for me. I use it either full-strength or diluted. I do not use any special brand or buy acrylic varnish except for bigger furniture pieces.

GLUE STICKS
Invaluable. But please buy good quality, branded ones, the cheap ones are rubbish and very frustrating to use.

STICKY TAPE
I use 'invisible' tape when I don't want it to show, and old-fashioned brown-paper tape when I do, which is available from hardware stores.

WALLPAPER PASTE
Used for papier mâché and decoupage techniques.

SHARP METAL SKEWER
I didn't realise how much I used this until I gathered a few of these projects together.

Other Tools

These are all a great investment and will be useful in your crafting.

FISHING LINE
For when you want an 'invisible thread'.

PAINT
Acrylic and/or watercolour.

FELT-TIPPED BLACK PENS

LIGHT SANDPAPER AND SMALL SANDING BLOCK
Ideal for taking off those little pesky edges.

BONE FOLDER
I discovered these after years of using a scalpel blade to score card and paper. It is, of course, made from bone, and is an elegant, flat, ivory-coloured object with a softly rounded point at one end. It scores not by cutting the paper fibres but by compacting them.

SMALL HAMMER OR RUBBER MALLET

HAMMER-HOLE PUNCH OR BRADAWL
A hammer-hole punch has interchangeable heads that attach to a metal tube. You position the head where you want the hole to be and then tap the end of the metal tube with a hammer or mallet to make a precise hole. It gives neater holes than a metal skewer.

NEEDLES AND THREADS
Sewing needles and thicker darning or canvas needles are always handy. Get some embroidery thread as well as cotton thread.

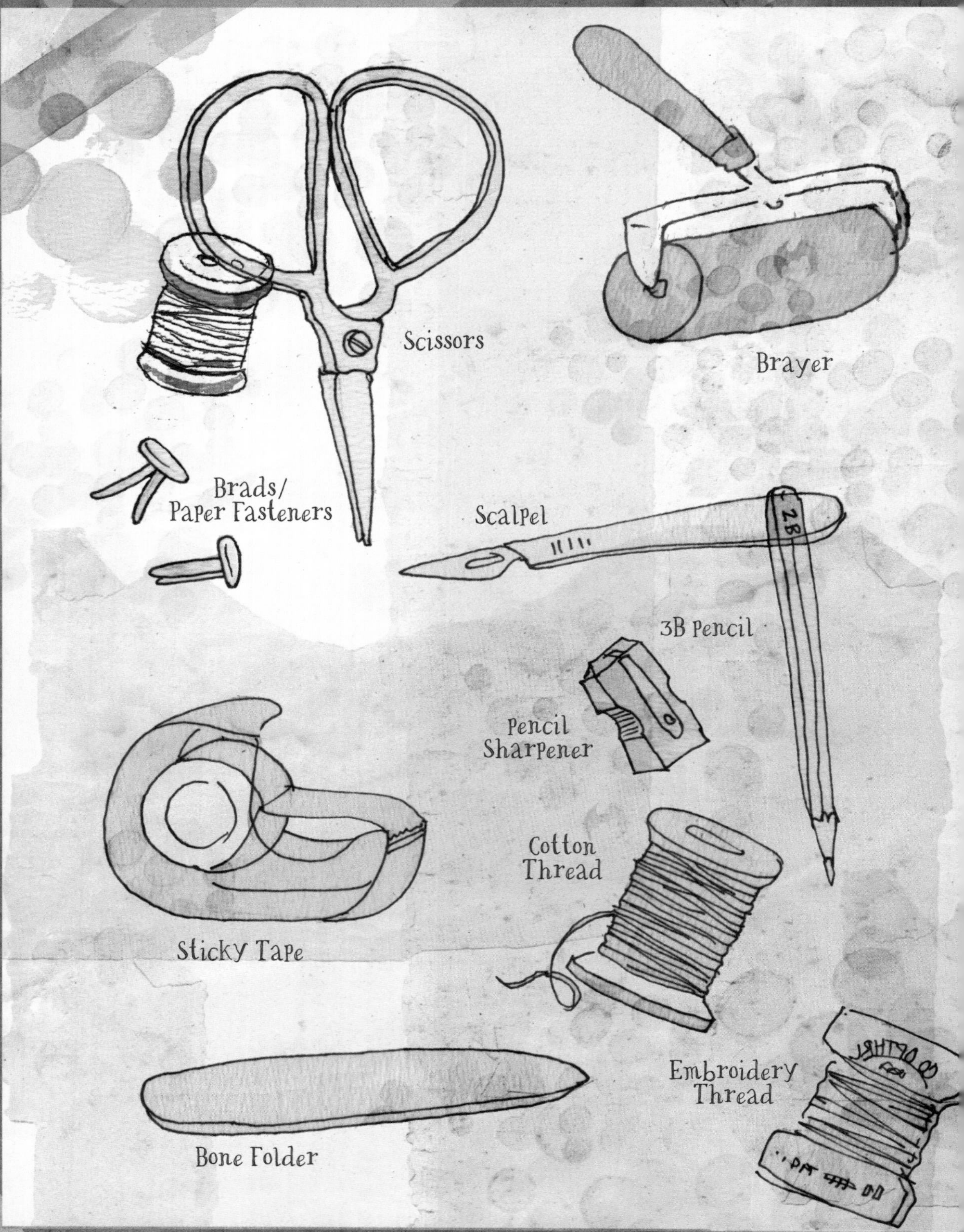
Scissors
Brayer
Brads/
Paper Fasteners
Scalpel
2B
3B Pencil
Pencil
Sharpener
Sticky Tape
Cotton
Thread
Embroidery
Thread
Bone Folder

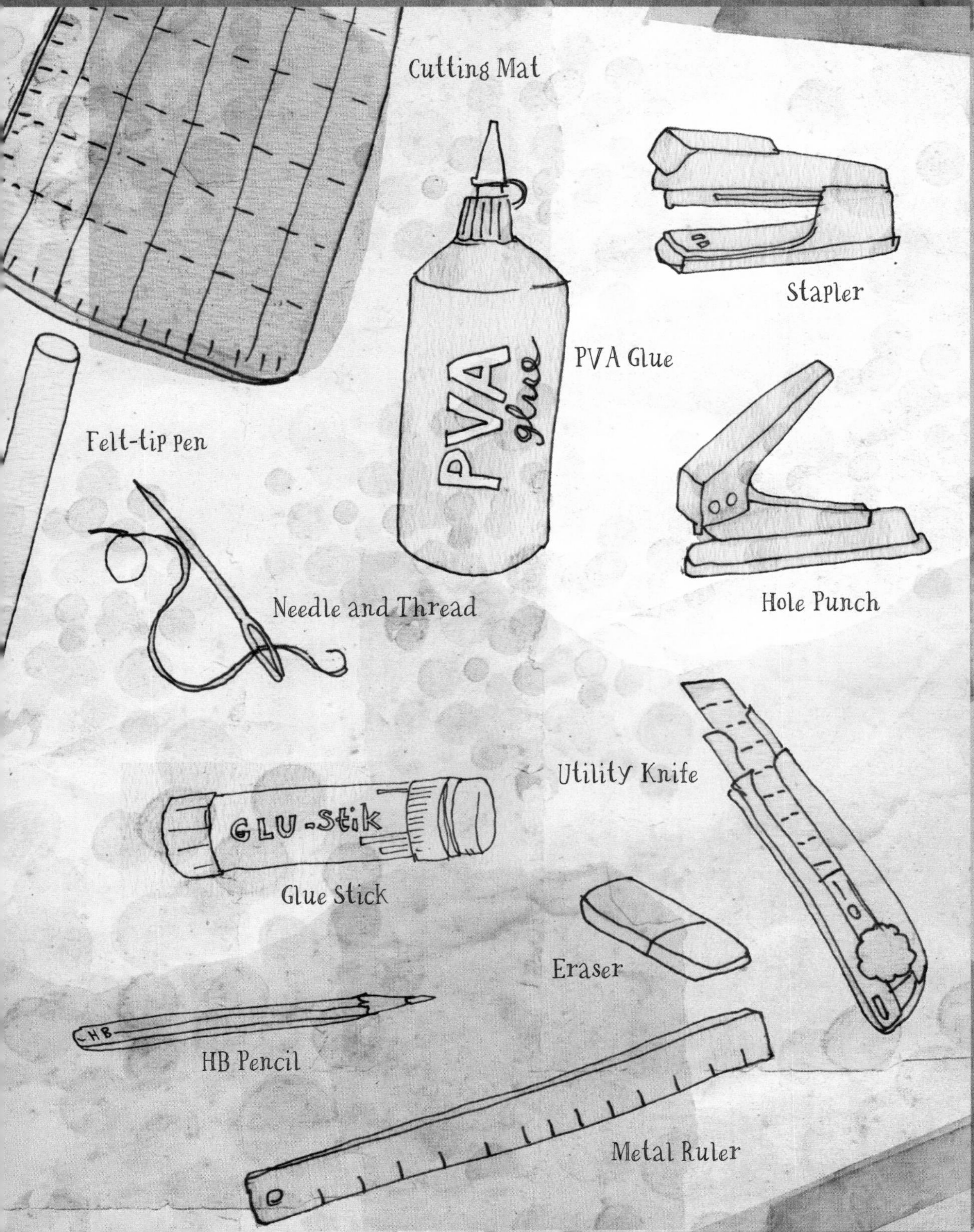
Cutting Mat
Stapler
PVA
glue
PVA Glue
Felt-tip pen
Hole Punch
Needle and Thread
Utility Knife
GLU-Stik
Glue Stick
Eraser
HB
HB Pencil
Metal Ruler

Techniques

PAPIER-MÂCHÉ

The Chinese are responsible for papier-mâché. The term actually means 'chewed paper'. The Japanese hijacked it to make their Noh masks and then the Europeans thought they'd get in on it.

In this book papier-mâché is the technique of applying many overlapping layers of torn-up scrap paper to make an object. (The 'chewed up paper' technique is where you make a pulp from paper and then mould it.) It can be done over an armature or mould (a humble bowl for example) and then sliced or 'released' using a barrier like petroleum jelly or cling film placed over the mould before the paper is applied.

DECOUPAGE

Of course you could guess it was the Italians who came up with this idea, about 300 years ago.

This is the method whereby you cut out images and glue them over an object and then apply varnish over the surface.

BLANKET STITCH

This stitch is worked from left to right. Bring needle up and hold the loop of thread down with left thumb. Make a vertical stitch as in diagram, bringing the needle out over loop of thread.

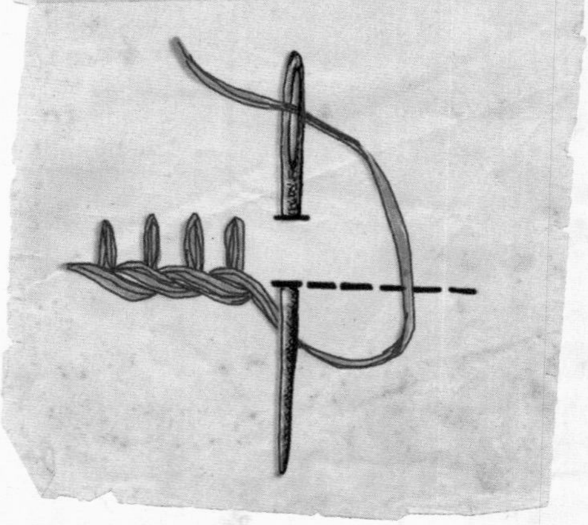

HOME MADE GLUE

If you wish to make your own glue instead of buying a pre-made one, here's a recipe that might take a little longer to dry than the manufactured variety, depending on the weather, but it holds really well with both paper and wood. Use an old paintbrush to apply it ... or use your fingers!

Ingredients

1 cup flour
1 1/2 cups water
1/3 cup sugar
10 drops tea-tree oil or 5 drops oil of wintergreen (acts as a mild preservative)

Mix the flour, sugar and water on the stove over a low heat until it thickens, stirring all the while to keep lumps from forming. Add the drops of oil, let it cool and then refrigerate in a screw top jar. It keeps a long time in the fridge.

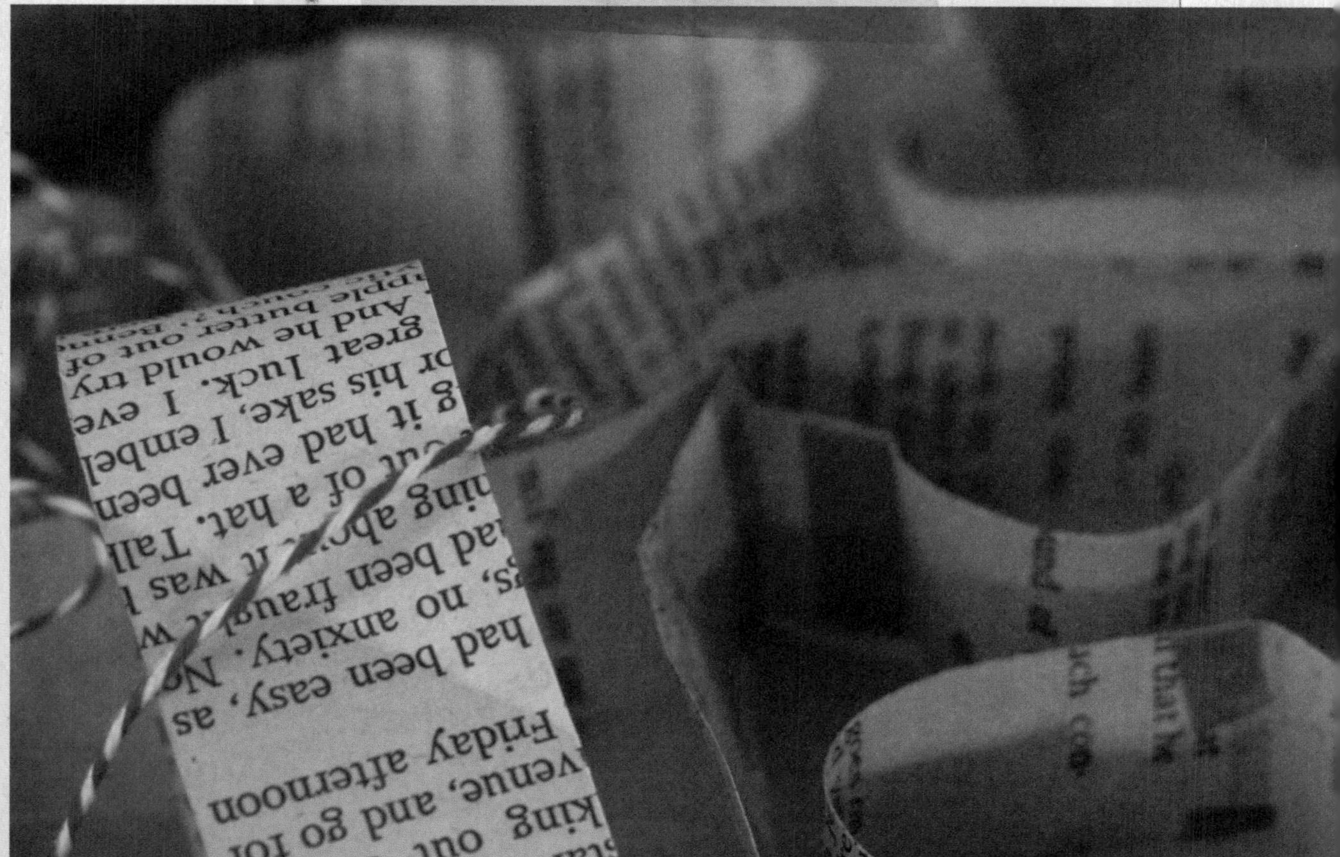

Ideas are like accidents,
you never know
when they will happen.

PIERRE VANNI — Designer

THERE
ARE NO
GARDENING MISTAKES
ONLY
EXPERIMENTS
JANET KILBURN PHILLIPS
RESULT
APRIL
2011
29 NOV 1935
THE
AUSTRALIAN
"HERALD"
LETTERS
EGYPT AND BRITAIN

EASY

Milk Carton Vases

My clever partner was the bright spark behind these sweet, inspired vessels. Because milk cartons are already waterproof, there is no need to worry about leakage. We ended up getting a bit carried away and covered about a dozen different sized cartons in all kinds of paper to see how they looked. What great presents they make, especially when you pop some fresh flowers into the spout.

You will be pleasantly surprised by the transformation of such a humble household item into such a lovely object.

YOU WILL NEED

Milk or juice cartons of different sizes

Patterned paper, enough to cover the cartons

Scissors, optional

Wallpaper paste, prepared to a yoghurt consistency

PVA glue

Small bowl

Disposable paintbrush

METHOD

1. Thoroughly wash and dry your cartons.

2. Cut or tear up your patterned paper into about 4cm pieces. Although, you can be very relaxed about the size and shape.

3. Dip the pieces of paper into the prepared wallpaper paste and apply to all the exterior surfaces of the carton. Use slightly longer pieces to cover the lip and inside of the spout, as you want the little bit of the interior that you see to look good too.

4. When the cartons are dry, thin some PVA glue with a little water in the bowl. Paint the exterior surface with 3 layers of the PVA mix, allowing each layer to dry before applying the next.

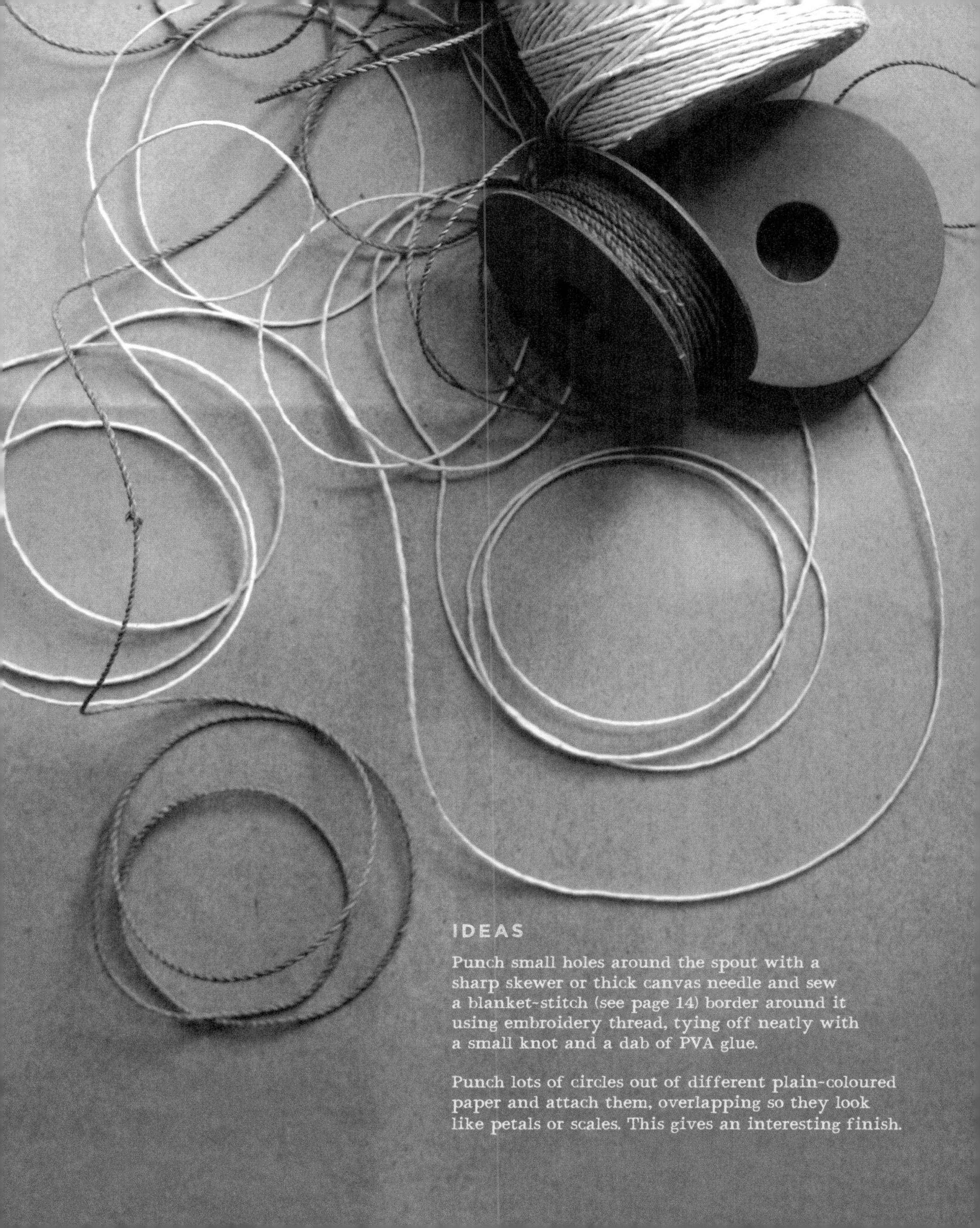

IDEAS

Punch small holes around the spout with a sharp skewer or thick canvas needle and sew a blanket-stitch (see page 14) border around it using embroidery thread, tying off neatly with a small knot and a dab of PVA glue.

Punch lots of circles out of different plain-coloured paper and attach them, overlapping so they look like petals or scales. This gives an interesting finish.

This is the toffee we love! What say you?
MACKINTOSH'S TOFFEE DE LUXE
ORIGINAL QUALITY
TOFFEE-DE-LUXE
ntosh's Toffee-de-Luxe
ust one sort of toffee,
are a good many sorts—
he list the other side
is tin.
y are all so deliciously
d that it is about impos-
le to fix on a favourite.
Plain T
Egg a
Mint-
Almo
Coco
De-
Ch
Al
Does the Drummer come to your house?
He is very busy all the year round in heaps and heaps of houses, giving old things new colours to make them look young again.
Drummer Dyes are just splendid for renewing faded, washed out frocks, and suits and overalls.
Choose your Colours from this list :—
Mary Blue
Light Blue
Saxe Blue
Royal Blue
Navy
Grey
Light Green
Dark Green
Emerald
Myrtle
Brown
Nigger
Tangerine
Red
Cardinal
Shell Pink
Pink
Old Rose
Pillar Box Red
Black
Daffod
Purple
Rust
DYES

CCXXIV CCXXIV

EASY

Papier-Mâché Bowl

I've been making papier-mâché bowls for decades, it seems. I regularly get a new burst of energy for them usually because I see some horribly expensive, beautifully patterned bowl or vase and decide I want to emulate it.

I used my own papers from my stationery line for these and was very happy with the outcome — nice and rich and opulent for something made from such humble materials, methinks! This is not a difficult project but there is a bit of waiting time for drying ... so do some other craft in the mean time.

YOU WILL NEED

Old newspapers

Scissors, optional

Small ceramic bowl

Petroleum jelly or cling wrap

Wallpaper paste, prepared to a yoghurt consistency

Patterned papers

Acrylic paint

2 small disposable paintbrushes

PVA glue (diluted with 50% water) to varnish

Metal skewer or hole punch, optional

Needle and embroidery thread, optional

METHOD

1. Roughly cut or tear the newspaper into 4cm squares.

2. Turn your ceramic bowl upside down on newspaper and slather it with petroleum jelly or cover firmly with cling wrap. I usually prefer the petroleum jelly option; though it leaves a film on the inside of the papier-mâché bowl, you can wipe most of this off with a paper towel afterwards.

3. Dip the pieces of newspaper into the wallpaper paste and apply all over the outside of the bowl, smoothing down the pieces of paper as you go — using your hands is kinda nice. Turn the bowl the right side up and make sure you go a bit above the rim, so that you have something to trim back to make a clean edge.

4. When the first layer is finished, let it dry a bit and then do a couple more layers in the same fashion. (I usually have a few bowls on the go at different stages, so I can work on some while others dry.)

5. Now cut or tear up your patterned papers. (I tried both cutting and tearing and liked them equally — they are just different kinds of looks.) Dip the pieces in wallpaper paste and paper over the newspaper until you have covered the whole surface.

6. Let the whole thing dry until it is bone dry. Depending on where you live and the weather, this could be a day or even a week.

7. Release the papier-mâché bowl from the real bowl, twisting gently if necessary to break any air seal that might have developed. (If it is really tough and not coming off, I have been known to puncture the bowl with a sharp scalpel point in order to release it.)

8. Take a look at your handiwork and trim off any daggy edges with scissors. (Or you can make a wave-like shape if you have enough edge to play with.)

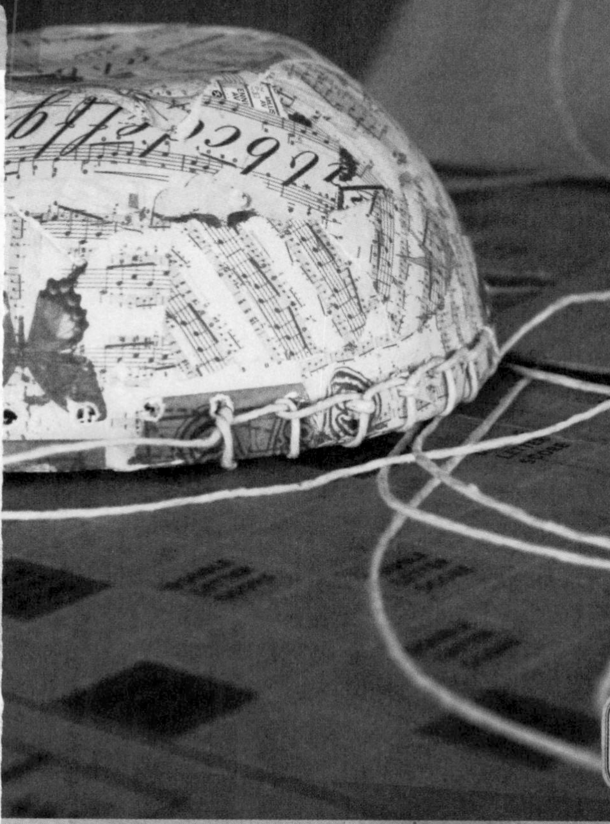

9 If you've used petroleum jelly, carefully wipe the inside of the bowl until it all comes off. I tend to wait a few days until the interior of the papier-mâché bowl dries a bit more before painting it.

10 Apply any colour you like to the inside, painting right up to the edges.

11 Now varnish it with the watered down PVA, as this does just as good a job as the more expensive acrylic varnish. Give it two coats inside and out, letting the first coat dry completely before applying the second.

12 If you're going to sew around the edges, do so after you've varnished and dried it. Puncture 7mm apart evenly spaced holes about 1–1.5cm from the rim using the metal skewer or hole punch. Using embroidery thread, sew a blanket-stitch border (see page 14) around the rim, then tie off with a small knot.

You're done!

IDEA

The stitching around the edge is, of course, optional, but I really love putting these two looks together. And the sewing neatens up the bowl's edge a bit. You could, of course, punch holes around the rim and thread string or whatever you like through the holes. You are probably better at sewing than I am, so you might be able to come up with something a little more interesting and challenging than basic blanket stitch. Go bananas!

My Dad, in our
'Jungle bathroom,'
circa 1972.

My mother decorated and used pattern flagrantly throughout the house, like a woman possessed. Thinking about it now, it occurs to me that none of the rooms matched, or even flowed easily from one to the other. Each room contained its own distinctive world, fashioned, it seemed, in, of and for itself.

The 1970s silver and green hexagonal wallpaper in my father's study is still there, so many decades later. It has gone in and out of style several times in that period. Funny, though, that it has never seemed wrong or anachronistic.

Of an evening as a teenager, I used to lock myself into Dad's study and play Rod Stewart and Peter Frampton albums over and over again on his turntable. As I disappeared into a reverie, minutely studying the artwork of the album covers, my image was sent back to me, distorted and skewed by the shiny parts of the wallpaper that covered the study walls. It was a glamorous world in there — with the low-hanging silver pendant light and the wallpaper that seemed to have a life of its own. It was a place that nurtured my growing sensibility; its atmosphere, light, colour and pattern mattered. These things were powerful, they could change a mood. In this highly decorated world, my spirit was set free, and I was anything I wanted to be.

TEMPLATE PROVIDED

MODERATE

Christmas Angel

These sweet little paper angels look gorgeous decorating a Christmas table, or strung up to make a mobile or hung from the Christmas tree. The great thing is that they require no glue or attachments, just some careful cutting.

YOU WILL NEED

Pages from an old book or sheet music for the back of the wings

200gsm patterned card, approximately A4 size, or laminate patterned paper onto a sheet of card by sticking them together with PVA, rolling over the joined sheets with a brayer to flatten, and then letting them dry

PVA glue

Brayer or rolling pin

Utility knife and cutting mat

Metal ruler

Hole punch

Kitchen string

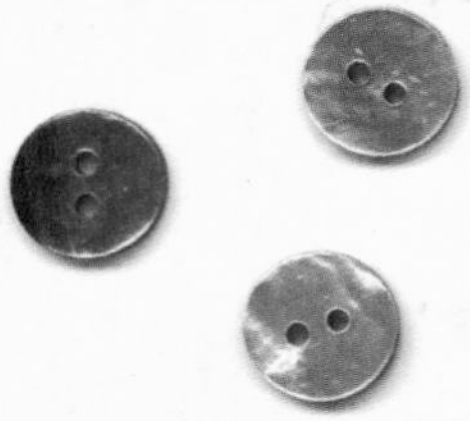

With hearty Greetings

Christmas

seasons greetings

With hearty

METHOD

1. First, stick the old book pages or sheet music to the plain side of the patterned card with a thin layer of PVA. Roll with the brayer or rolling pin to remove any wrinkles or air bubbles. Allow to dry.
2. Transfer the template, which is on the inside of the book's jacket, onto your card.
3. Using your utility knife against the metal ruler cut the straight edges first. Pay extra attention when cutting the slots where the wings will be inserted.
4. You're on your own with cutting the curves! It's best to make them in one or two sweeping movements to avoid a ragged outline. Make sure you accurately cut under the arms. I made a few angels that weren't cut under the arms enough, so the angel didn't curve properly when standing up.
5. When you've finished cutting, hitch the wings up and insert into the slots. Then with a hole punch, make a hole in the head, thread through some kitchen string and hang your angel on the tree, or simply stand her up to watch over Christmas festivities.

Hark, hear the angels sing!

IDEAS

Give the angels faces. The angels I modelled these on have dear little closed eyes and a halo of hair in a semicircle ... paint these on or cut up some decorative paper to make the facial features and adhere with a glue stick.

You could also cut more of a patterned shape into the wings, but be careful to keep the angel balanced on both sides, or she will lose her balance.

seasons greetings
180084

Dream By The River
It's Good To Be Queen
Paris
Holiday Gift Tags
Package of 10
HKG
JFK
FRAGILE
CLT
UIE

Pinboard Inspiration

I don't know about you, but I love photos of other people's pinboards. They are so revealing and intriguing!

I keep an ever-changing pinboard with a flurry of inspirational stuff pinned to it. Sometimes I find buried treasures hidden for maybe a year or more by bits and pieces I've pinned on top.

Keep a pinboard and pin those things on it that you haven't had time to put in a notebook. Or, if you're like me, you might want each new inspiration to have its time in the sun, so display it in front of your desk for a spell, then move it to a notebook later.

Whatever you do, collect and keep bits and pieces that inform, delight and surprise you.

You will find they will eventually make their way into your art and craft projects one way or another.

MONARCH
CHICAGO
WATKINS
PURE
CAMPHOR
BALM
Hat Pins
TABLET
SONGSTER
NEEDLES
CANTON
GINGER
E.C.RICH, NEW YORK
OF BEST
ENGLISH
MADE

EASY

Book Sculpture

I spotted this idea in a gallery in New Zealand, where the artist had made dozens of these from different kinds of books — some with fresh white pages, some yellowing and old. They were gathered randomly across one wall and looked very impressive — as though, if you listened carefully, they might have a lot to say. For something so simple, they sure looked both complicated and sophisticated. I was intrigued and had to go home and attempt them. Turns out they were only the latter.

Making these is very meditative — I guarantee that after one, you will be hooked, and want to make more. My partner's seven-year-old son had quite a thing for making them for a while, and steadily made his way through several books to create a cornucopia.

YOU WILL NEED

Lots of old books, paperbacks are best. If you choose hardbacks, strip them of their covers and save them for making the covers of the Vintage Journal project

Double-sided foam tape, for hanging

METHOD

1. Start on the first page and fold the bottom half of the page to make a triangle (see photos below). Do the same to the top half of the page. You should now have a triangular page, the point facing right. Continue folding each page this way until you've done every page.

2. When you've finished, apply double-sided foam tape at a few spots on the back of the book, and attach your book sculpture to the wall. Make a few so you can create an interesting configuration, or leave them sitting on the mantlepiece to make a decorative shelf sculpture.

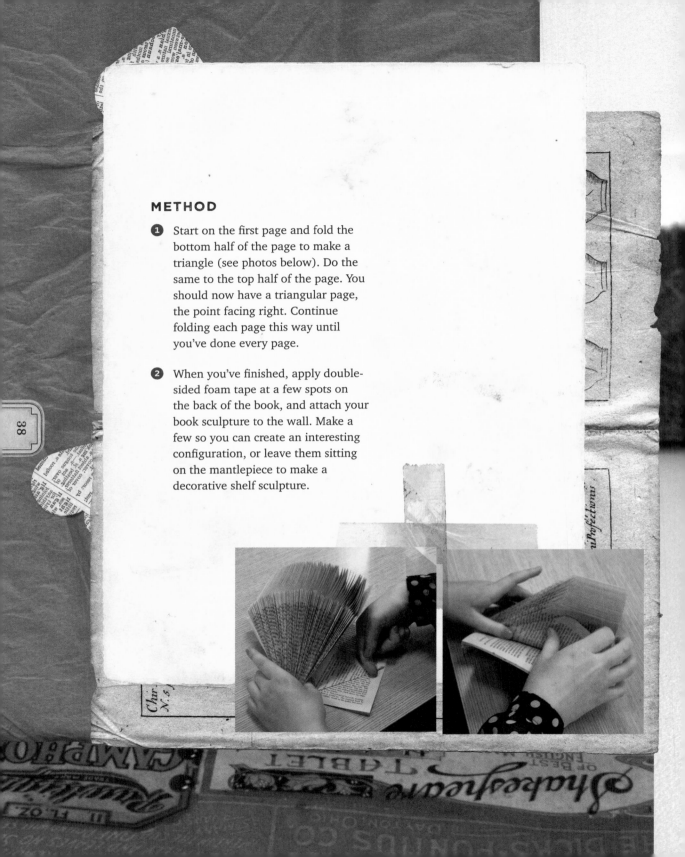

IDEA

You can cut shapes into the pages once they are folded, but be careful as you risk undermining the strength of the whole piece, making it fragile.

Use colour swatch books; different types and weights of paper make for interesting sculptural edges when folded.

RISTMAS
963

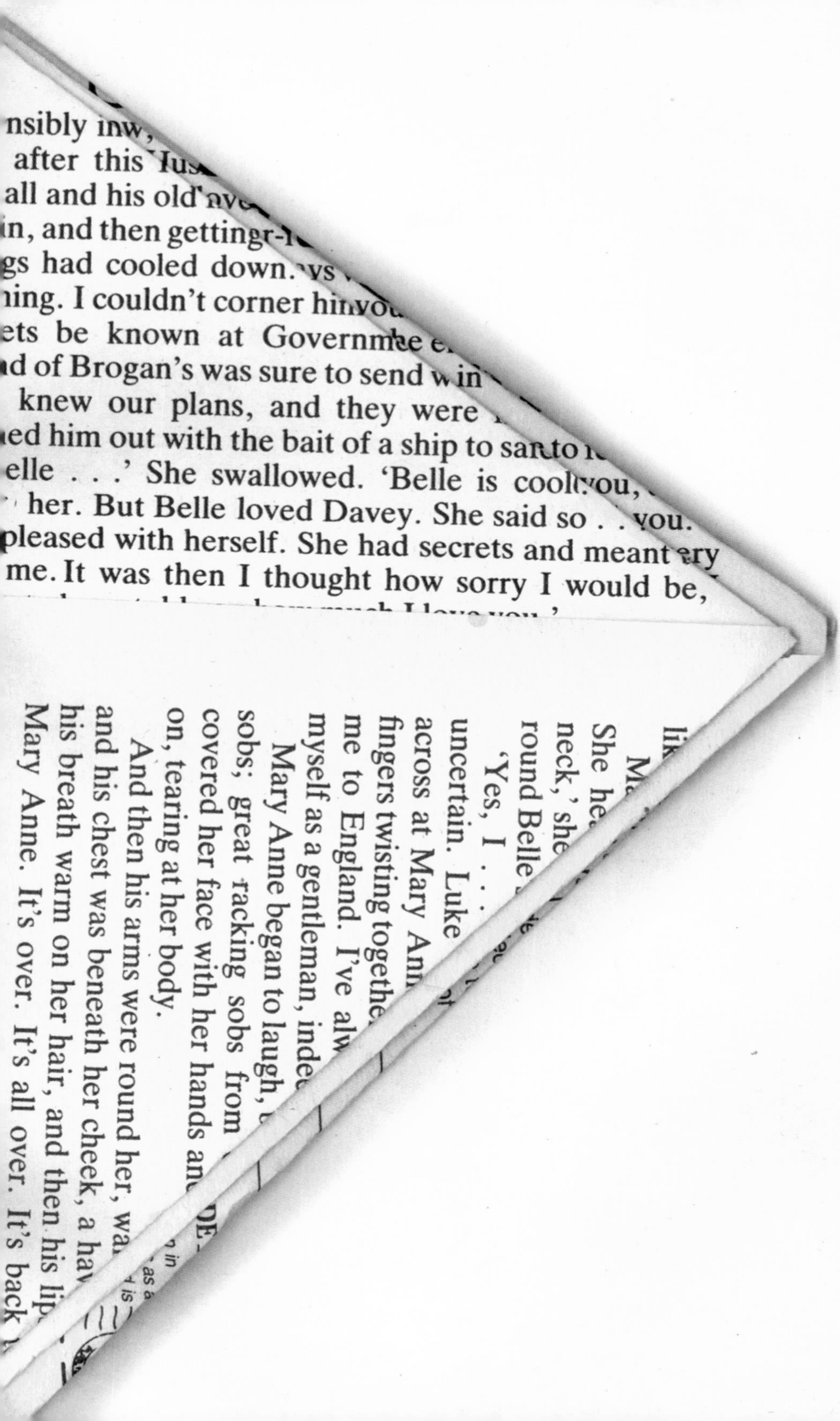

nsibly inw,
after this
all and his old
in, and then getting
gs had cooled down.
ning. I couldn't corner hi
ets be known at Governm
d of Brogan's was sure to send
knew our plans, and they were
ed him out with the bait of a ship to sa
elle . . .' She swallowed. 'Belle is cool
her. But Belle loved Davey. She said so . . you.
pleased with herself. She had secrets and meant
me. It was then I thought how sorry I would be,
round Belle
'Yes, I . . .
uncertain. Luke
across at Mary Ann
fingers twisting togethe
me to England. I've alw
myself as a gentleman, inde
Mary Anne began to laugh,
sobs; great racking sobs from
covered her face with her hands an
on, tearing at her body.
And then his arms were round her, wa
and his chest was beneath her cheek, a ha
his breath warm on her hair, and then his lip
Mary Anne. It's over. It's all over. It's back

intoned the robot in a metallic
admit no one until I return, Alphonse!"
patted the robot on the shoulder
to the chalet overlooking the moonlit valley
over his overalls, clamped a hat on
on to the verandah. The door
humanoid robot.
work and electronic gadgets
in an hour, Alphonse!" he
overnment are in

PAR AVION
VIA AEREA
TOM
AIR MAIL

I watch as my partner's small children take to the paper I hand out to them with scissors and hole punches at the ready. Their faces are full of glee.

The little one presses the wooden stamp letter block so deeply into the peacock-blue ink pad, I fear it might never be retrieved — ink bleeds up around his fingers and I know each and every one of those little digits is destined to wear the stains for days. They seem to become almost one with their projects: *I am what I create.*

Within half an hour, everything and everyone is stamped, quite as though we are in some mad 'kindy' tattoo parlour. Oh, how we love to cut and stamp!

How divine is this simple togetherness. Such a timeless pleasure is this: a glue stick, some paper scraps, crayons, an ink pad — some imagination.

ENFAN

IDEA

MODERATE

Little Paper Boxes

Little boxes: I find them irresistible. There are many things you can do with them and they are perfect for small homemade presents. These are a bit fiddly but the lovely result is well worth the effort. Take care with your measurements, the more accurate you are at the start, the better the result. But if you're like me, and don't have much of an eye for a straight line, you can always slice off excess bits of the overhanging paper later.

TEMPLATE PROVIDED

YOU WILL NEED

A3 sheet of 280gsm card

Utility knife and cutting mat

Metal ruler

Bone folder

A variety of patterned and/or coloured papers

Spray adhesive

Newspaper sheets

Brayer or rolling pin

PVA glue

METHOD

1. Transfer the template, which is on the inside of this book's jacket, onto your card.

2. Using your knife and the metal ruler, carefully cut around the outline. Score the dotted lines with the bone folder, or if you don't have one use a utility knife to cut halfway through the card so the card folds easily.

3. Fold the scored lines and you will see you have a box shape. Unfold the card again, so that it is flat. For each side of the box choose a piece of patterned paper and cut 6 pieces to size.

4. Lay the pieces of paper face down on large sheets of newspaper and spray adhesive lightly but thoroughly on to the back of the pieces (do this outside as the fumes are quite toxic).

5. Now stick the pieces of decorative paper into place on the flat box. Use the brayer or rolling pin to really stick them down and remove any air bubbles. Leave to dry, and then re-fold your box.

6. To keep the box from unfolding, strategically place a few dabs of PVA glue.

7. With a sharp blade, trim any excess paper overhanging the edges of the card.

IDEA

You may want to use Japanese washi tape, or something similar, on the edges of your box if you are not happy with them. This will also add an extra dimension of colour and pattern, and give the box more strength. If some of the card is showing through, you can colour it in with Textas or crayons.

Faithful and true
SCALLOP
SHAPES OF SHELLS
COMMON MUSSEL
PERIWINKLE
SEA EAR
CW 3254
SINGLE
FAVOURITE FLOWERS
TUCK'S POST
CARTE POSTALE
POST CARD
Be sure y
Sold by Lea
Lanman
K-100-K
50 Kronen 50

CENTIMES
1915
LES CHANSONS
STEREOTYPES
RONDES
LES PETITS ENFANTS

COLOUR

Colour, I have come to realise, is so central to our aesthetic experience of the world. Whether you're into a low-key or high-key palette, arresting or more comforting colours, there is always the happy possibility that you can still be surprised by how colours can enhance, dramatise or harmonise with each other.

In my design work, I have been made to realise that I definitely go through periods of pinks and greens together, and then have a batch of minimal blacks and whites — quite as if I were trying to balance the colours out, give them all a run. With a newly hatched batch of artworks in front of them, I will sometimes overhear someone saying, 'Skye's obviously going through one of her pink and green periods!'

I tend towards warmer hues and have trouble with cyan or peacock blues. I don't know why. But what I do know is that the colours you are attracted to are deeply built into you, and you will reach for them time and time again. This is, I believe, a sign of your innate style. Expressing it in your intimate surroundings can be such a joy. Don't fret too much about colour — you have your own particular sensibility, and if you're unsure, just ask a friend, perhaps, about what colour they think you like best. It can be quite revealing!

Use colour with impunity in your craft and art projects. Layer it and see how it changes when different hues are laid on top of one another. Juxtapose colours that you wouldn't normally put together and see what happens. Do they need a 'bridge' colour — something to make them relate to each other maybe? Do they need breaking up with linework or pattern?

You will always be drawn to your usual colour habits, but sometimes the artwork can use just a bit of what you never thought it would: cyan or purple among the usual pinks and greens ... Surprise yourself!

he saw two men.
TRAVELLING

EASY

Puzzle Piece Brooch

I love a brooch. Even though I don't often wear them, I collect them avidly. Here is a great idea using old jigsaw puzzle pieces — many are just the right size for a brooch. I was lucky to find pieces that were die-cut into interesting shapes in a two-dollar jigsaw I found in an op shop: an elephant, a plane and a gingerbread man ... what luck!

I covered them with some pages from books and lacquered them, or stamped them with alphabet stamps. These make such interesting and unique gifts — and you can go that step further and put them in a little box that you have either found and altered or made and decorated.

YOU WILL NEED

Old books, manuscripts, sheet music

Old jigsaw puzzle pieces

Glue stick

Utility knife and cutting mat

Brayer or rolling pin

PVA glue

Brown kraft paper

Brooch fasteners, available from craft stores

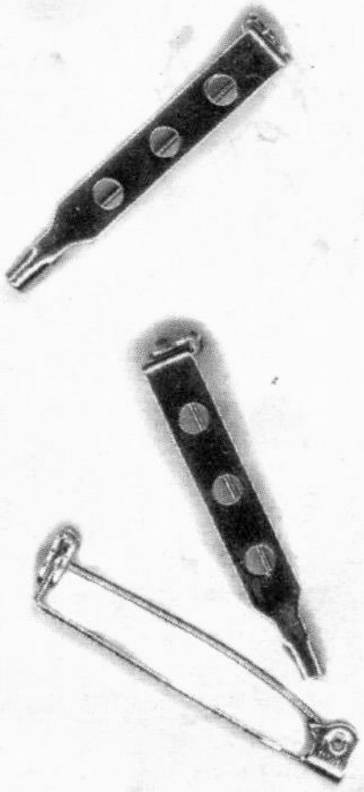

METHOD

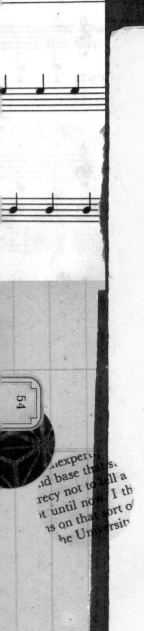

1. First, cut out interesting bits and pieces from old books or music sheets that you like the look of and that have patterns or designs that generally fit with the shapes and sizes of your jigsaw pieces. (I had lots of fun cutting up words and rearranging them into random sentences that ended up having their own kind of poetry. Tailor them to suit the receiver … you will be amazed what interesting and random stuff you come up with once you get going with the scissors.)

2. Select which bits of paper work best with your jigsaw pieces. You can use a number of pieces for each jigsaw piece to build up interesting effects.

3. Using the glue stick, apply the glue to the back of each piece of paper and to the surface of the jigsaw, and attach. Don't get too worried about slight ridges or overlaps. Any paper hanging over the edges can be trimmed off later when the glue is dry.

4. Using a brayer or rolling pin, place a piece of scrap paper over the surface of the puzzle piece and gently but firmly roll it back and forth, securing and flattening the collage onto the puzzle piece. Leave to dry.

5. Trim off any pieces of overhanging paper with the utility knife by holding the jigsaw piece firmly face down on a cutting mat. It will take a few goes and will be quite fiddly cutting into any rounded corners. When you are satisfied with the edges, turn the piece over and have a look at your handiwork.

6. Now glue the brown kraft paper onto the back of the jigsaw piece either using the glue stick or a thin layer of PVA glue. (Too much PVA glue makes the paper buckle, too little glue stick will cause the paper to peel off.) Let it dry. With the kraft-paper side face down on a cutting mat, trim off the over-hanging brown paper with your utility knife.

7. To attach the brooch fastener, squeeze out a thin line of PVA glue along the middle of the back of the jigsaw piece. Don't worry if there is excess glue, as this can be used to varnish the back, but try to make the glue line straight and even. Carefully place the brooch fastener into the line of glue and press down firmly for a minute or two. Leave it to dry.

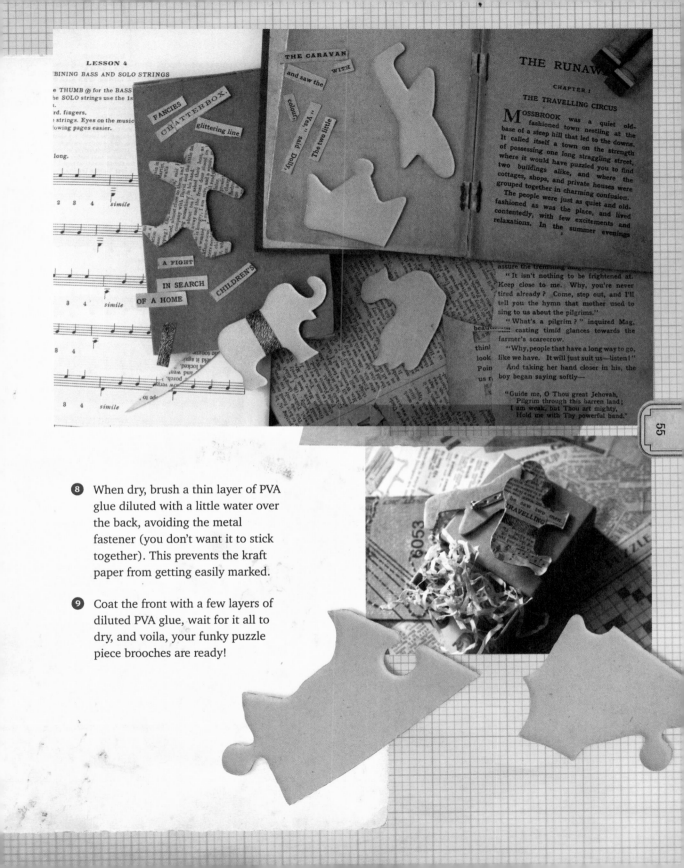

8. When dry, brush a thin layer of PVA glue diluted with a little water over the back, avoiding the metal fastener (you don't want it to stick together). This prevents the kraft paper from getting easily marked.

9. Coat the front with a few layers of diluted PVA glue, wait for it all to dry, and voila, your funky puzzle piece brooches are ready!

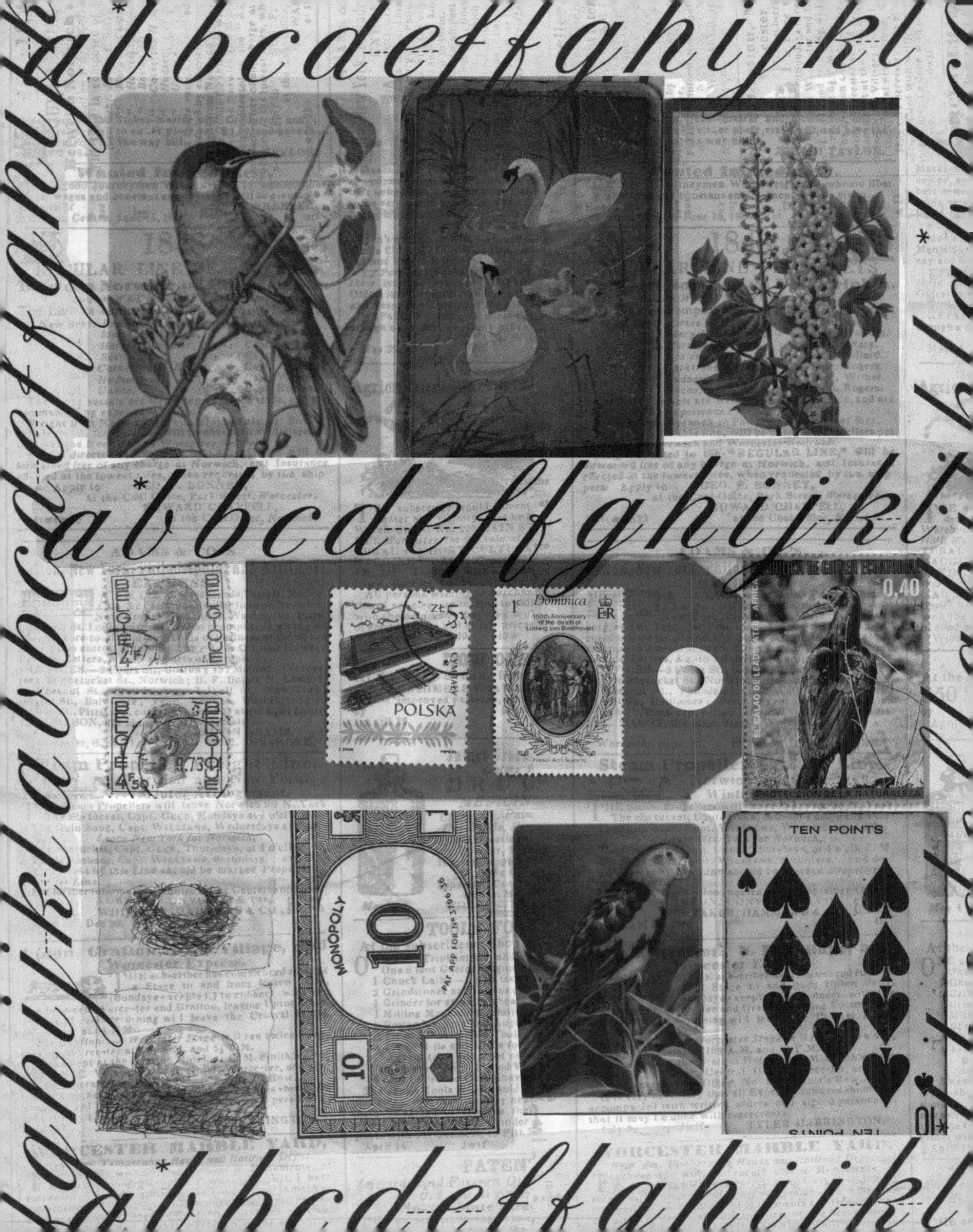
abbcdeffghijkl
abbcdeffghijkl
abbcdeffghijkl
ZŁ 5
POLSKA
Dominica
150th Anniversary of the death of Ludwig van Beethoven
BELGIË
BELGIQUE
PROTECCION DE LA NATURALEZA
0,40
MONOPOLY
10
TEN POINTS
WORCESTER MARBLE YARD

Bowerbirding

We all borrow. Inspiration comes from so many places, it's virtually impossible not to be influenced. When I first started out on my creative journey I used to try and copy exactly what I saw before me. Whether it was something in 3D or another person's drawing, I tried to record it exactly. At the age of 12 or 13 I was obsessed with Farrah Fawcett and drew the most ubiquitous image of her face over everything. I ended up doing a metre-square painting of her – one of my very first sales. This was good practice. I learned techniques this way – how to make acrylic paint look like airbrushing, for example.

I am curious about processes. I used to spend a lot of time (and still do) wondering: How did that clever person render that wash so beautifully underneath that pen sketch? How did they tear that piece of paper to fit into that space so perfectly? How did they have the patience to ...

Copying is a sort of compliment to the original artist, a way to try to get inside another's head.

So don't shy away from it or be embarrassed that you feel the need to 'copy' sometimes. You will find your own way through it and inevitably develop a style that's very much your own. Even though you might not realise it, you do already have a style. It is just waiting to be developed, to be seen for what it is.

AIR MAIL

PULL
RECORD
BOND
Xx
HOUGHTON-BUTCHER
(Great Britain) Ltd
High Holborn, London, W.C.1
Wills's Cigarettes
1848
NEAT WORK
10
Jump your bunny right along
You get ten hops. Ding-dong!
Ding dong!
MILK
RAW

MODERATE

Yuletide Dove

This is another clever Christmas decoration that just requires careful cutting. I was inspired to create this dove after browsing through a book of 3D paper-craft instructions.

YOU WILL NEED

280gsm blank card, approximately A3 size, or laminate patterned paper (for example, Christmas paper) onto a sheet of card by sticking them together with PVA, rolling over the joined sheets with a brayer or rolling pin to flatten, and then letting them dry before cutting

Utility knife and cutting mat

Bone folder

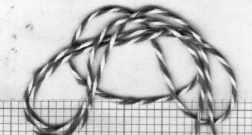

christmas greetings

METHOD

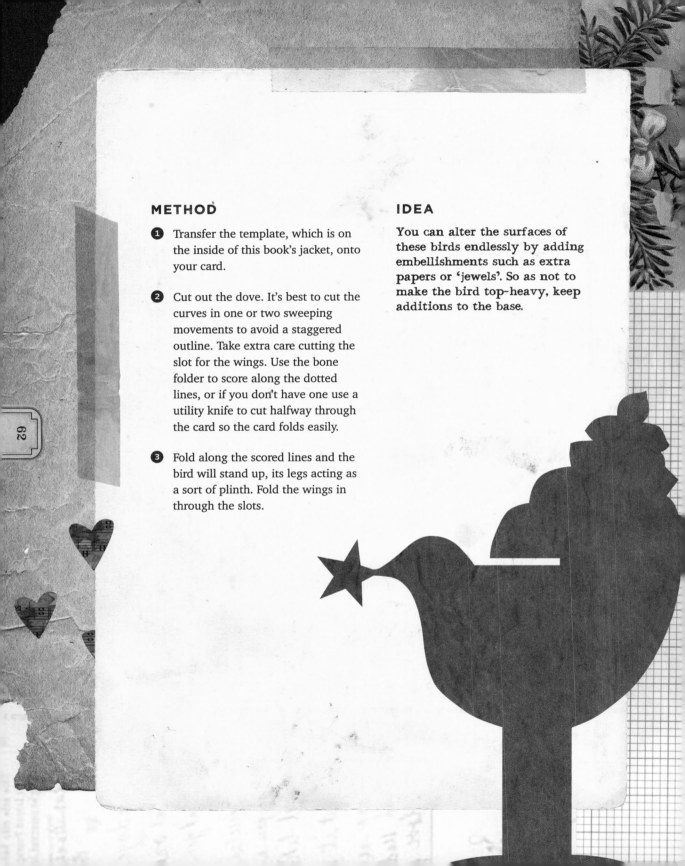

1. Transfer the template, which is on the inside of this book's jacket, onto your card.

2. Cut out the dove. It's best to cut the curves in one or two sweeping movements to avoid a staggered outline. Take extra care cutting the slot for the wings. Use the bone folder to score along the dotted lines, or if you don't have one use a utility knife to cut halfway through the card so the card folds easily.

3. Fold along the scored lines and the bird will stand up, its legs acting as a sort of plinth. Fold the wings in through the slots.

IDEA

You can alter the surfaces of these birds endlessly by adding embellishments such as extra papers or 'jewels'. So as not to make the bird top-heavy, keep additions to the base.

CHRISTMAS WISHES
POST CARD
merry christmas
45 London Rd
merry christmas

zu sein. — Auf
ommer gemietet, sollte
begab sich dahin. In der
er Italiener von recht häß=
n Sitten, der bemühte sich
andern entfernte
auf und ab
Lippen.
drückte er
nicht, und
rderben!"
nd ihn traf
Schauer erregt
widrige junge
us, von Eifersu
nde Reden gege
Man
sich ein
und noch häßl
Giulietta und
Ingrimm sich
Seitenalle
chte ihn
ein?"
erzeit innern
6.00 Was
(PG, R)
(CC) 6.30 Escape Fro
(CC) 7.00 News On 3.
Trapped! (CC) 7.35 Dance Academy.
8.00 Vampire Knight. (PG, CC)
The Next Generation. (PG,
Diary. 9.00 Close.

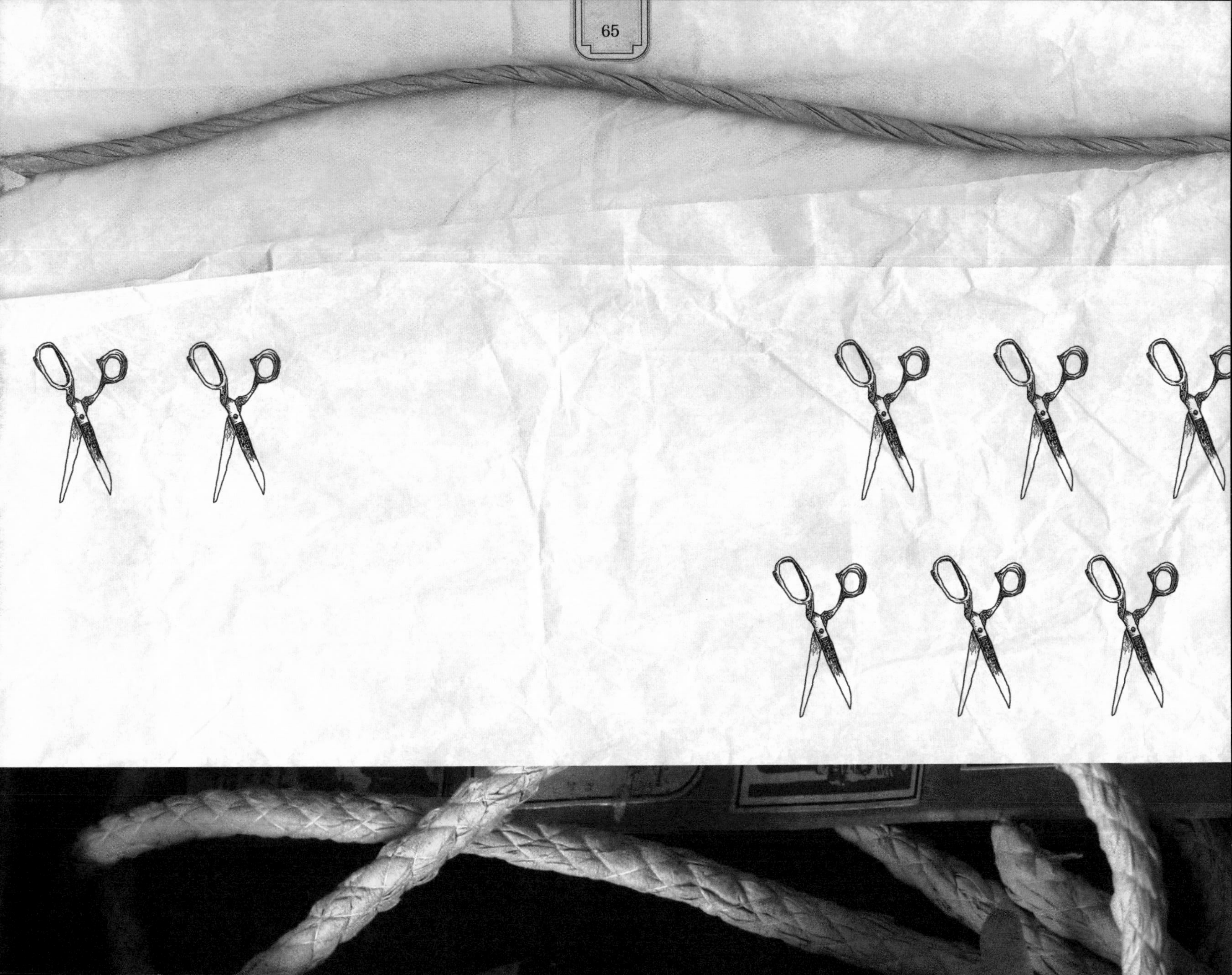

EASY

Petite Pictures

I did these while on a farm holiday — hence the nest and nature theme. A very simple idea, with so much room for variety. They look great gathered in small batches on a wall ... and can be personalised too.

YOU WILL NEED

Utility knife and cutting mat

Metal ruler

Cardboard — you can use pretty much anything. It's best if it's heavier than 280gsm, however, as it gives the pieces more ballast. You can even use standard box cartons that are hanging around and destined for recycling.

Some pages from an old book (the older and yellower the better)

Coloured images — mine were cut from approximately 280gsm coloured board, but thinner is probably better, so they don't look quite so raised or bulky from the side.

PVA glue

Brayer or rolling pin

Glue stick

Scissors

Hanging mechanisms, with framing or jewellery wire

Tin snips

MANDU
1
2
3
4
68
UMPA
RIET
ILLINOIS CENTRAL RAILROAD CO.
GOOD FOR ONE PASSAGE BETWEEN
And
57431
Only on suburban trains on date of purchase stamped on back. Subject to tariff regulations.
Form S.B.G.
Passenger Traffic Manager
TRAVELLERS' TALES.
THE VISIT
20
MALAYA SELANGOR
CARDIFF

METHOD

1. On the cutting mat, cut out a piece of cardboard with the utility knife and ruler so that it is a little smaller than the size of your book pages.

2. Wrap a book page around the piece of cardboard, moving it around until you are happy with the placement of the text. Ensure the page hangs over the edges of the card so it wraps around to the back. (Though this is not essential, it does create a nice neat look.) Remove the page.

3. Slather the cardboard with some PVA glue, lay the page over it and gently press it down. Use the brayer or rolling pin to firmly press the pieces together. Let it dry for 20 minutes or so. To neatly wrap the overhanging edges to the back of the cardboard, mitre the corners at the four edges by tucking the paper under itself, as you would when wrapping a present. With the glue stick, glue these bits down, and if necessary, place the whole thing under a heavy object overnight to ensure it all stays put.

4. Cut out and glue one or more coloured images to the covered cardboard using the glue stick, which I find is less messy for this process than PVA glue. Roll over with the brayer or rolling pin to make sure the images are firmly attached and won't curl. Wait for them to dry, then add a wire attachment to the back of the cardboard and a small length of wire to hang your petite artwork. If you wish, throw a lick of PVA diluted with a little water over the front and sides of the image to add a little protection and gloss, or leave it, as I did, matt and ready to weather.

With seasons
Greetings

I ended up making about 10 different kinds of houses when I started making these, and always with someone in mind — music and flowers for my mother, swallows and stamp patterns for a friend who'd just moved. They look so gorgeous lined up along a shelf. Cutting the windows out (or not) will make the light that travels through the little houses interesting at different times of the day, especially if you use a coloured paper for the interiors.

I had mine placed so that the afternoon sun streamed through them — and indeed, one could imagine whole little worlds going on inside those paper houses.

EASY

Paper Houses

These little houses are a delight. They are basically a cutting and scoring exercise, so if children are involved, they will have to be carefully supervised. You can customise the houses in so many ways: use any bought or found heavyweight card to fashion them, and add bits and pieces to their exterior surfaces after assembly. You may even want to make some paper people to live in them.

YOU WILL NEED

Lightweight patterned paper

2–3 sheets of 280gsm card, available from art-supply stores, or any heavy weight card you have around the house. You will need about an A3 sheet per house, depending on how big you want your finished item to be.

PVA glue

Disposable paintbrush

Brayer or rolling pin

Utility knife and cutting mat

Metal ruler

Bone folder

Invisible sticky tape

Embellishments, optional

TEMPLATE PROVIDED

METHOD

1. Attach your lightweight patterned paper to the heavyweight card with PVA glue, rolling over the joined sheets with a brayer or rolling pin to flatten, and then let them dry overnight under a heavy book.

2. Transfer the template, which is on the inside of this book's jacket, onto your card.

3. Using the metal ruler to guide, carefully cut the lines around the perimeter of the house, deciding as you go which of the windows you want to remove or leave open. If you want them to open and close, cut through the top, bottom and one side but score the fourth side, so that the window can be folded open.

4. Use the bone folder, or if you don't have one use a utility knife, to cut halfway through the card so the card folds easily.

5. You will now be able to start folding along the scored lines. Use a dab of PVA to hold the sections in place. (Or if you're like me and impatient for it to dry, use invisible sticky tape. You won't be able to see it once the house is finished, as it will be inside. However, it can be tricky once the house is nearly enclosed — there is no easy way, I'm afraid, but to persevere — I use a pen, or the end of the utility knife if it is small enough, and poke it through the windows to press the last few edges together.)

Your house is now ready to occupy!

IDEA

I tried a 'blank' model, with just white card and the scored lines. My neighbour, who watched while I was in the process of assembling the house, loved the plainness of the white house ... which goes to show that my particular fondness for pattern on pattern isn't to everyone's taste! Vary your patterns — or even lose them altogether for a clean and very modern look.

IDEAS

Make a whole town! You can photocopy the template and scale it up or down — although the smaller it gets the fiddlier the work involved. I like to break up the intensity of the patterns and colours, keeping some houses plainer while others are busy with detail.

If you want to make quite a large house, you can easily attach different sheets of card together. This way you can also have fun using different patterns on each panel of the house.

THE END OF MARRIAGE
True North
BRIGHTNESS FALLS
AMOS OZ
IAN McEWAN
Here at The New Yorker
Pacific Pearl
PASSAGES FOR MEN
ANTIPODES
Overreachers
SUN UNDER WOOD
WHY I WRITE
AGAINST
The Factory
Life's Like That
Mothers
GILEAD
What I Think I Did
PROZAC
Country Life
HAL PORTER
MARK SANDERSON
THE HOURS
THE RITES OF PASSAGE
BITTER LEMONS
On Lies, Secrets and Silence
THE OTHER SIDE OF YOU
SALLEY VICKERS
The American Replacement of Nature
Australian Publishing Program 2007
IAN McEWAN
MARTIN AMIS
SELF
DAVID LODGE Therapy
CHARLES HANDY
CAROL SHIELDS
SHORT CUTS
The Disappointment Artist
The Love~Me Bird
LATE BLOOMERS
BRENDAN GILL
MARTIN AMIS EXPERIENCE
HANIF KUREISHI THE BODY
GARDENING
KURMA

Keep a Library

Along with my obsession for paper, I am a great collector — some would say hoarder — of books. While all books are precious to me, I literally swoon in the design section of book stores. But it's not just 'designy' titles that catch my eye. What's so lovely is that design has so thoroughly infiltrated what used to be fairly dry-looking tomes. Pick up any book now and someone will have gone to quite some trouble to impel you to do so — the paper used, the way it is bound, the addition of a special flap or some amazing use of colour, all show that consideration of the physical object is still premier in this digital age. What we see and touch matters — we have an emotional response. So it is that ideas and inspiration are everywhere — you just have to look. Book stores are the proof then, if it is needed, that the book — and its corresponding paper — are not dead.

As it happens, I keep a not-so-little tribe of books circulating around the house. (The nice thing is that they look so very lovely stacked in their wobbly rows about the place. A kind of beautiful paper artwork in themselves. Well, I think so anyway!)

It often astonishes me that I haven't noticed the amazing design on, say, page 202, or the idea inherent in the small box in the bottom-right corner. Just moving a book from halfway down the pile to the top can reveal pages and pages that fuel my inspiration. We find, I think, what we need, when we need to. Books are not just a one-off inspiration investment, they continue to reward. If you can't afford to buy them, borrow them. Or do what I sometimes do, and find a little stool you can pull up in an aisle of your favourite book store and flip through the titles on offer, taking notes, maybe doing some sketches, all the while inhaling the lovely scent of fresh paper ... Heady stuff!

COMPAN

EASY

Bird Mobile

This gorgeous paper bird mobile makes a wonderful homemade present for a friend or for a child's nursery. As well as looking great, it is a way to get young kids to learn the names of different kinds of birds.

Decorate the white board however you please; I just liked the simplicity of the black and white theme here.

TEMPLATE PROVIDED

YOU WILL NEED

80gsm patterned paper (optional), approximately A4 size

280gsm or heavier card, or buy ready-made blank white animal cut-outs from art-supply or craft stores as I did

PVA glue

Brayer or rolling pin

Utility knife and cutting mat, or scissors

Paints, pencils, pens or paper to decorate

Sharp metal skewer and a block of old wood

Fishing line

Bamboo or balsa wood struts 40–50cm long to hang birds from

String

METHOD

1. If you are using patterned paper, attach it to the card using a thin layer of PVA. Roll with the brayer to smooth it out and remove any air bubbles. Allow to dry.

2. Transfer the template, which is on the inside of this book's jacket, onto your card.

3. Neatly cut out each bird shape using a utility knife and a cutting mat, or use good, sharp scissors.

4. If you are using plain card without patterned paper, decorate both sides of your birds with stamps, coloured pencils or however you want.

5. Punch a small hole into the top of the head of each bird with a metal skewer and the block of wood.

6. Cut the fishing line to various lengths so that the birds hang at different heights and can twirl around each other. The longest should be 40–50cm long. Thread the fishing line through each hole and tie a small knot to secure.

7. Assemble the struts at right angles to each other and lash them together with string. Attach a loop of fishing line to the centre so the mobile can be hung from the ceiling or a doorway.

8. Tie the birds to the struts, adjusting their positions so they are balanced and you are happy with how they are flying.

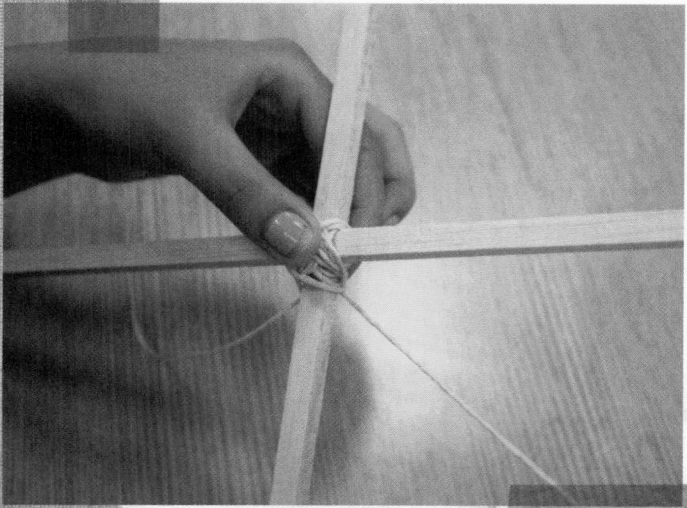

Creativity is all in the art of looking — of perception. When in doubt, check out the supermarket aisles, the local recycle bins, the bottom of your handbag. You will be amazed at the inspiration you find there.

So many of these projects can be achieved in a lunchtime, or an afternoon, some may take you the best part of a weekend. If you're anything like me, you may leave your projects lying about the place so you can stop and look at them from time to time, or check on them in a different light, in different parts of the house.

Something that might once have seemed *tres ordinaire* on the sideboard can surprise you by working extremely well next to the couch. It's all about the relationship between things.

resently, in a
always
poetry
of two souls
used to tell me. "I want to know everything
bout you: all y thoughts, all your dreams, all your secrets
give yourself to me completely
gazed across the roo
end, her
idn't ever marr
not.' Anna a heavy
uring it with steel wool
anything more terrible than being complet
person. Or owning them. That's wh
h another
se you w
he unmi
shes to
. . . If y
oice trai
wool o
She finis
glanced
said.
nished
s she set it
Practis
Oh, Anna,' Celia said wit
impatient. 'That's just becau
different when you're in love.'
'Maybe
laughed.
Celia's
known
nothing.
room.
brought

EASY

Paper Necklace

Another great use for the mail that comes through your door each day! I call these 'contemporary temporary jewellery'. They won't last forever, of course, but even the scrunching and bumping of wear and tear makes them more interesting. And you can make them out of different papers for different occasions or to match various outfits. If giving as a present, they look great in a box with some more shredded envelopes inside.

YOU WILL NEED

Strips of the same width of torn-up envelopes folded to make concertinas

Metal skewer and a block of old wood

Hammer or rubber mallet

Smooth string or thread about 80cm long

Thick embroidery needle, optional

A few beads, optional

METHOD

1. Scatter your concertina strips of envelopes over a flat surface to make it easy to spot the shades and colours you have at hand.

2. Gather the concertina strips in a pile of approximately 3cm pieces. Hold the pile together firmly on the piece of old wood and punch a small hole through the centre of the pieces of paper using the metal skewer and the hammer or rubber mallet.

3. Feed your string or thread through the hole. I just eased the end of the string through, but if you're having difficulty, you might want to use a blunt embroidery needle to help you.

4. Repeat the process, gathering up your strips, punching a hole and threading them onto the string until you have enough paper to make a necklace. If you're using beads, thread them either side of each batch of paper to keep the paper in place and to add a bit of sparkle.

5. Loosely tie a bow or knot to fasten.

IDEA

If you really want to be irreverent, use old bills and/or bank statements. If it's over seven years old, you could even use your tax return.

You can also use more formal methods with your paper, of course. Try folding lengths of paper in various ways and threading string through these, perhaps adding a few fringed pieces too. They can end up looking quite delicate and lovely.

Make an unusual bracelet. Just keep threading pieces of paper until you have enough for a bracelet, then tie the ends together with a small knot. The knot should remain hidden under the froth of paper.

If you have leftover Christmas wrapping paper, you can always do a Christmas-themed version. Tear or cut up your paper into squares and follow the instructions above ... any kind of paper can work, really.

THINGS YOU CAN DO WITH YOUR
PAPER COLLECTION

Fold it up,
stick it down.
Cut it, slice it,
punch holes in it.
Scrunch it, iron it.
Wet it, dry it.
Roll it into balls.
Tear it.
Bend it.
Crease it.
Pull on it.
Twist it.
Smooth it.

MATCHES
BRONCO BRAND
SAFETY MATCHE

MATCHES
n Sweden fo
LE STORES
Special Quality
TRADE MARK
MADE IN SWEDEN
SAFETY MATCHES
SAFETY MATCHE

29

EASY

Heart Wreath

This is a bit like an elaborate, large-scale paper necklace. It's amazing what you can achieve with some leftover Christmas paraphernalia.

Christmas tissue paper and odd bits of Christmas wrap can be employed to make this year's delightful door wreath. Though this is a simple project, it takes some time to thread the paper onto the wire, so go slowly, and do it as the urge takes you.

YOU WILL NEED

1m (approximately) coathanger-gauge wire or an unravelled coathanger

Tin snips

Big bunch of wrapping and tissue paper scraps, torn roughly into approximately 4cm squares

Metal skewer and a block of old wood

Hammer or rubber mallet

Small craft pliers

METHOD

1. Make your heart shape by gently bending the coathanger or wire into shape. Snip off any unwanted length. Leave the ends of the wire free so you can thread the paper onto them.

2. Gather about a 3cm stack of your bits of paper (any thicker and it's hard to get the skewer through), alternating different patterns and types of paper, so there is variety in each batch. Squash the batch down on top of the old block of wood. To make a hole through the batch, punch the skewer with the aid of the hammer or rubber mallet, through the centre of the pile of torn paper.

3. Carefully thread each batch of paper onto the wire, trying to keep the shape of the heart as much as possible while not crushing the pieces of paper too much. When you have threaded enough paper onto the heart to fill up one side, start threading from the other side of the wire heart. At this point, don't push the pieces of paper together too much as you want them to 'flutter' a bit. Fluff the pieces apart a little as you go. It is a balance between exposing too much of the wire frame and having the pieces of paper too crammed together. You will find a happy medium as you go along and can always rearrange the placing of the paper squares afterwards.

4. When you have reached the other end of the wire, coaxing the papers around the soft top curves of the heart, stop. Using small pliers, loop one end of the wire around the other end of the wire heart. The finished wreath doesn't need a hanging device as I found it hangs quite nicely just resting on a door knocker.

IDEA

You could fashion any number of shapes from the wire for your wreath: a star, a dove, a bell or a tree. Just remember though, the more curves or edges it has, the more difficult it is to get the papers around those corners.

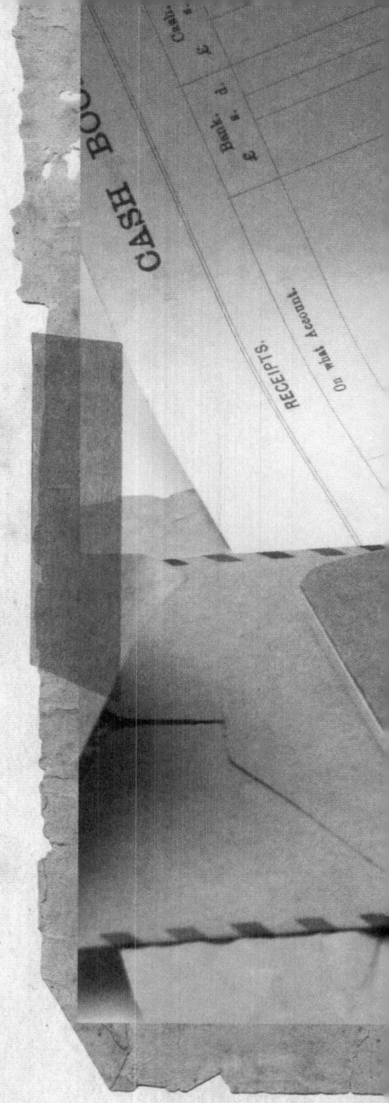

Notebooks

Keep a notebook as a visual diary. Or if, like me, you have a tendency to misplace it, have several. I have one in the bedroom drawer, three in the office, another languishing in my handbag and still others I know not quite where!

Stick things into them that appeal to you — bits of paper, tickets, menus, leaflets, dockets. Use them for scribbles, notes and descriptions. There's no pressure; no one need ever see them. What will begin to emerge is a kind of sensibility. Perhaps unbeknown to you, your eye is often drawn to certain things: reds or blues, fonts and lettering, paintwork or leaf shapes. By recording what appeals to you, you will arm yourself with a treasury of goodies to dip into. Not only that, you will start to connect the dots. If you look carefully at what you collect, your strengths will begin to reveal themselves. If you find it difficult to analyse your finds objectively (I confess that I can find this quite difficult), hand your notebook over to a trusted friend and have them tell you what they see in it. If they don't say 'a whole lot of junk', then you're onto something. If they do, then ask someone else!

I also take photographs, often just with my mobile phone, but at other times I go out to discover the neighbourhood with my nice, big, posh camera. What I have uncovered is interesting ... and has taken me a while to analyse: *I love house numbers.*

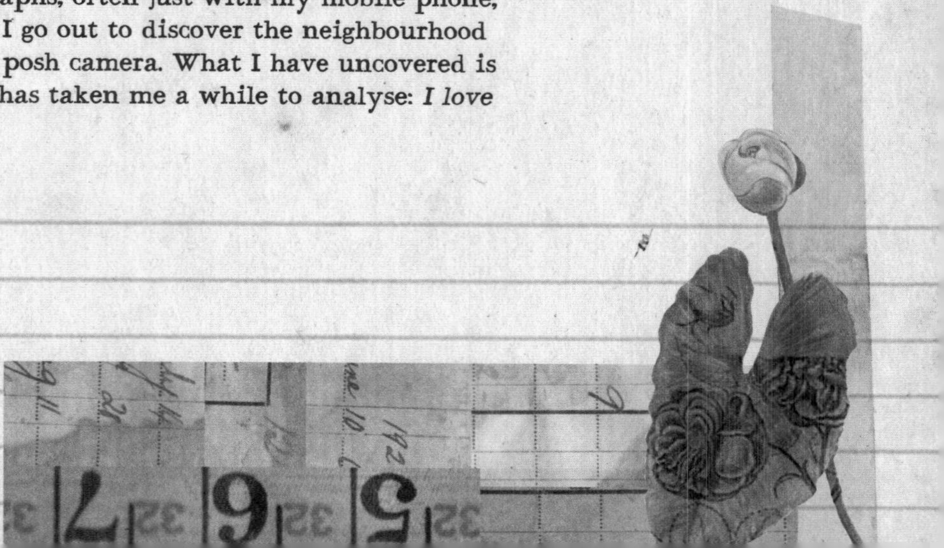

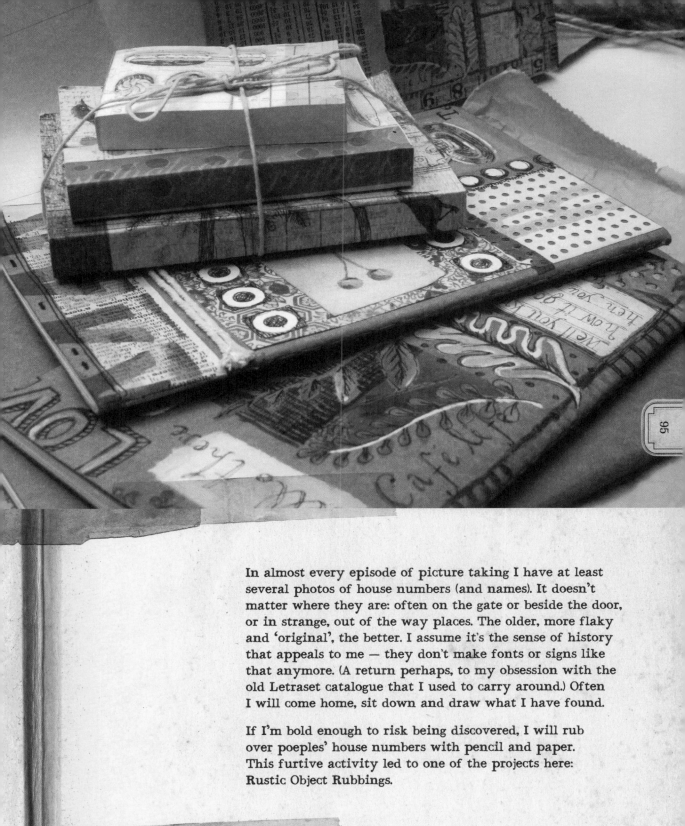

In almost every episode of picture taking I have at least several photos of house numbers (and names). It doesn't matter where they are: often on the gate or beside the door, or in strange, out of the way places. The older, more flaky and 'original', the better. I assume it's the sense of history that appeals to me — they don't make fonts or signs like that anymore. (A return perhaps, to my obsession with the old Letraset catalogue that I used to carry around.) Often I will come home, sit down and draw what I have found.

If I'm bold enough to risk being discovered, I will rub over poeples' house numbers with pencil and paper. This furtive activity led to one of the projects here: Rustic Object Rubbings.

THE SMALL HINDOO PEN
MACNIVEN & CAMERON, LTD

MAHATMA GANDHI
EXERCISE KALUM
PEN
No. 6B
No. 6B
M.M.KADERJI & Co.
ABDUL RHEMAN St. BOMBAY.
MADE IN ENGLAND

EASY

Little Envelopes

I don't know about you, but I'm a bit of a stationery nut … that's one of the reasons it is such a pleasure to run a card and stationery business. I especially love envelopes: little ones, big ones, lined, blank and/or patterned ones. You might end up making dozens of these as they are so cute and so very handy for keeping things in or sending out to friends for little thankyous.

YOU WILL NEED

A4 sheets of 80gsm paper, or printed paper

Utility knife and cutting mat

Metal ruler

Bone folder

Glue stick

METHOD

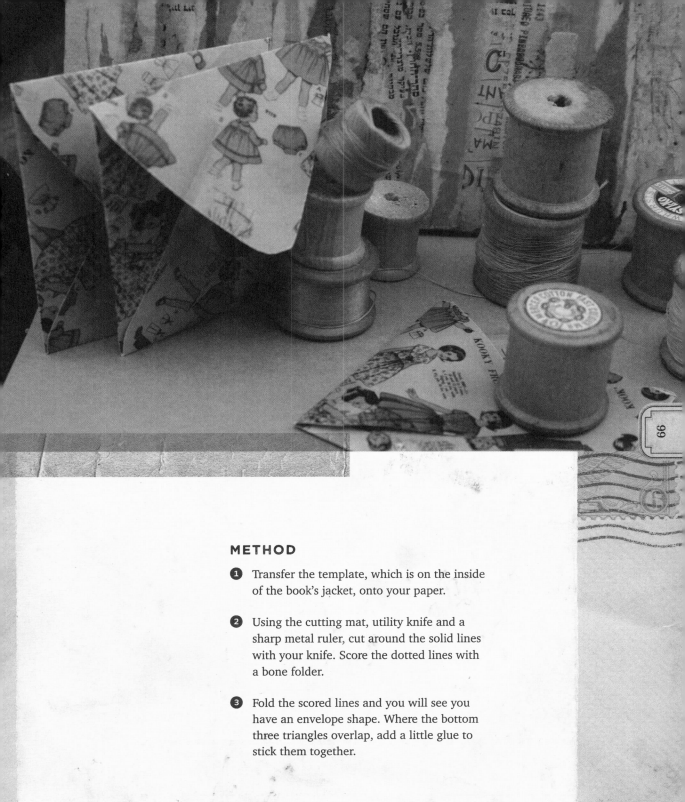

1. Transfer the template, which is on the inside of the book's jacket, onto your paper.

2. Using the cutting mat, utility knife and a sharp metal ruler, cut around the solid lines with your knife. Score the dotted lines with a bone folder.

3. Fold the scored lines and you will see you have an envelope shape. Where the bottom three triangles overlap, add a little glue to stick them together.

IDEA

You can always glue on some extra flourishes or decorative elements pertinent to the receiver. Another lovely idea is to fashion an interesting closure — stitch or use brads (paper fasteners) to attach another piece of shaped card or memento to your envelope.

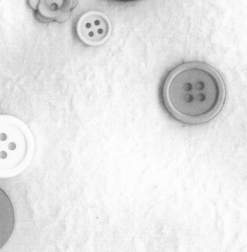

These FREE Patterns Enclosed
The World Over — It's The 'Kooky' Look!
1/6

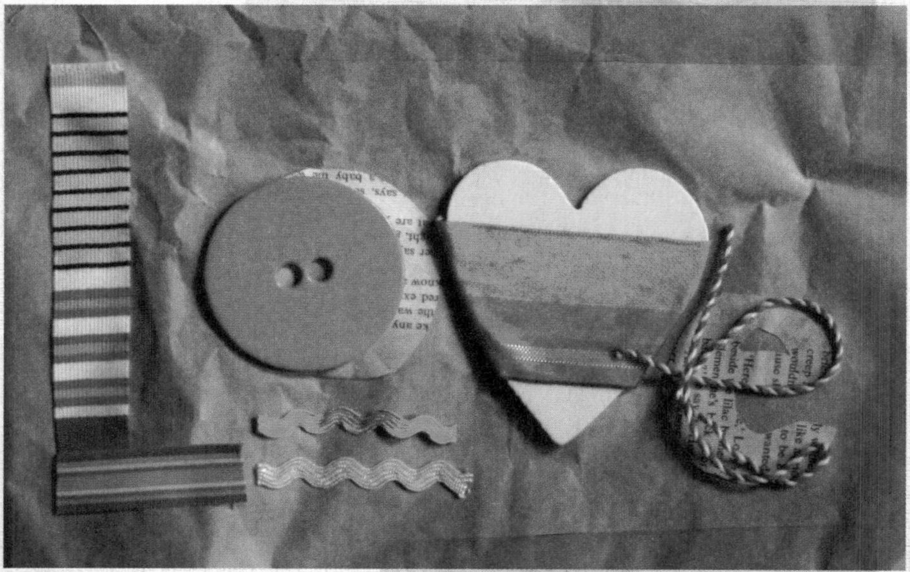

Creativity

I'm ashamed about many things, especially about the inabilities and deficiencies I have. I can't, for instance, draw hands or feet — even cartoon ones — very well. They always end up looking like club feet or mittens. I have absolutely no idea of perspective. I cannot draw straight.

Perhaps, as my friend Chris (who is great at drawing hands and feet) says about this issue of mine, it's just that I'm not paying enough attention or concentrating hard enough to fashion what I'm seeing into a competent image. But it is probably both more and less than that.

Creativity is a strange beast. Almost nothing I create is resolved the way I might have expected it to be.

The process of creating is not linear. It has taken me forever and a day to recognise that my deficiencies are also, exactly, my strengths. My mistakes, my artistic misdemeanours, give my lines, doodles, cut-outs and vistas a personality. They make what comes out of me incorrect and imperfect but unique. Sound familiar? And though I often still rail against it, I have learned to harbour a quiet respect for my mistakes — through them I have developed images and objects that I, and sometimes other people, love.

So I squabble with those who say, 'I can't draw such and such'. Or, 'I can't sew'. And for those who claim not to be creative ... give them a glue stick, some paper and tell them they've got an hour to come up with something, and they will usually be amazed at what they discover about themselves.

It's a confidence trick, this creativity business.

SOUTH
AMERICA

EASY

Native Bird Card

Making rough or cartoon images of native fauna is great fun. It also gets the kids thinking about representing what's around them rather than the usual ubiquitous dinosaurs. I was in New Zealand on a holiday and we came upon the famous Pukeko bird — and had great fun fashioning the shapes for his body and feet.

This project is perfect for travelling — with a few simple tools you can make these just about wherever you go. I keep a little bag with me in the car containing just a few crafty bits and pieces for just such times. (Just make sure you also pack the GPS, as someone might get quite cross when they find their map has been cut up for a craft project.)

YOU WILL NEED

A piece of 200gsm card

Backing card 280gsm, optional, this card should be twice as wide as the card above, it can also be in a contrasting colour so that your card has a colourful border.

Bone folder

Decorative paper (when travelling I used colourful sections of the local newspaper and local maps)

Utility knife and cutting mat, or scissors

Pencil

Set square or ruler

Glue stick

PVA glue

Brayer or rolling pin

Needle and sewing thread, optional

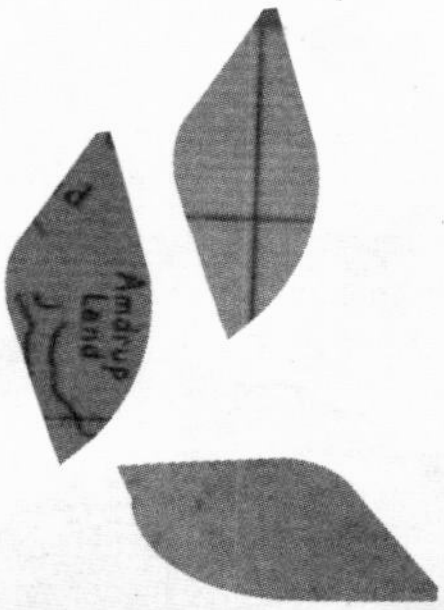

METHOD

1. Cut the card to the size you want. If making a card that opens and closes, cut a backing card so that it is 5mm larger on all sides (for the border) and twice as wide. Score the backing card down the middle with the bone folder.

2. Choose your papers ... the fun bit!

3. Using a pencil, roughly draw the shape of a local animal or bird onto your paper. If it's a bird, try cutting out the main body shape from a map and cutting pieces from magazines or newspapers for its feathers to add texture and interest. If it's an animal that has scales or an unusual head or paws, use different papers to highlight these.

4. Play around with the image and see how well the patterns work together — or not. You may have to cut out several feathers or feet from magazines before you are happy with the layout.

5. Stick the pieces of paper down onto the card using your glue stick then roll with a brayer or rolling pin to flatten. Let them dry.

6. If you want to stitch around the animal or bird, do so now, but make sure the glue is completely dry otherwise your needle won't go through. First make evenly spaced holes around the edge of your animal using your needle, and then thread the needle and sew around. I use a double thickness of fine sewing thread. Finish by tying a knot at the back.

7. If you are making a card that opens and closes, attach the card to the backing card with either PVA glue or a glue stick, making sure the corners are well stuck down. You should now have a border on all sides.

8. If you want to add a button or any other decorative element, do so at the end. Stick it down with PVA glue — this is the best way to attach it as a glue stick might not be strong enough.

IDEA

If you prefer, this can be just a large flat piece of artwork to be mounted and hung on the wall

Old Letters

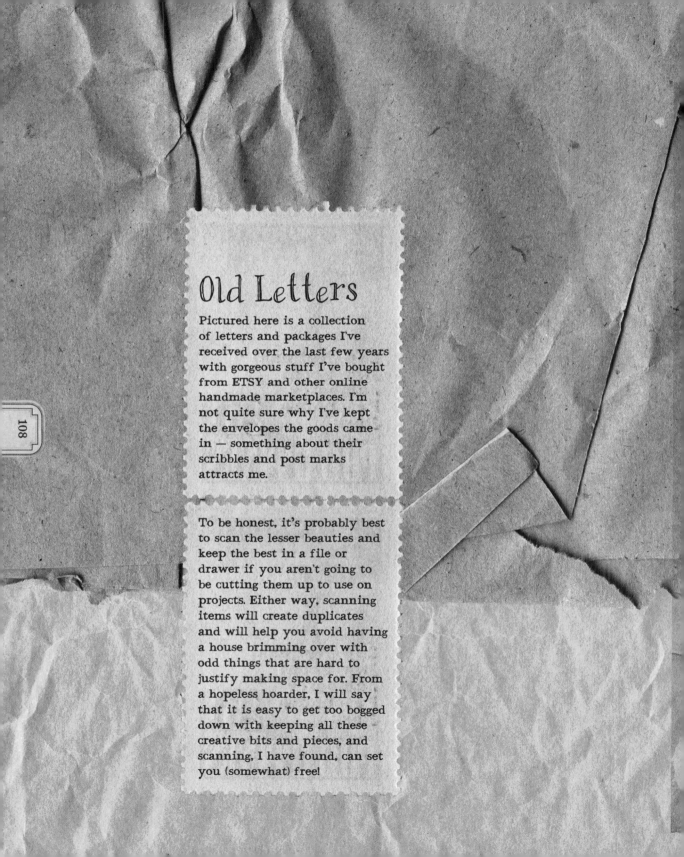

Pictured here is a collection of letters and packages I've received over the last few years with gorgeous stuff I've bought from ETSY and other online handmade marketplaces. I'm not quite sure why I've kept the envelopes the goods came in — something about their scribbles and post marks attracts me.

To be honest, it's probably best to scan the lesser beauties and keep the best in a file or drawer if you aren't going to be cutting them up to use on projects. Either way, scanning items will create duplicates and will help you avoid having a house brimming over with odd things that are hard to justify making space for. From a hopeless hoarder, I will say that it is easy to get too bogged down with keeping all these creative bits and pieces, and scanning, I have found, can set you (somewhat) free!

Sushipot Art Objects
57 Calais Street
EPOCA
TAMPA
MADE IN
TRADE SILVER TIP MARK
PULL
3c USA
U.S. POSTAGE
PAID
CEDAR RAPIDS,IA
52401
SEP 08 07
AMOUNT
$7.20
00052092-23
UNITED STATES POSTAL SERVICE
Po Box 602
Oakland CA 9463
USA
USA 41
Pittsburgh
USA
AIR MAIL
U.S. POSTAGE
PAID
HOPEWELL,NJ
08525
AMOUNT
$0.84
00018799-03
Skillman, NJ 08558
USA
TO SKYE ROGERS
Sydney NSW
Australia
PITTSBURGH PA
USA
USA 1¢
Skye Rogers
Sydney NSW
AUSTRALIA
AIR MAIL
2039

MODERATE

Petal Lampshade

I love this lampshade. There are so many different ways of personalising it ... using white or coloured papers for example. But I like the way the brown kraft paper throws a warm amber light when the lamp's switched on, and when it is turned off, the lampshade is like a funky piece of paper art. It would also look good on a longer-limbed lamp base.

YOU WILL NEED

Frame of cylindrical lampshade

Brown-paper tape 35mm wide

280gsm card for making petal templates and the discs for the back of the flowers

12 A4 sheets 80 gsm brown kraft paper or other lightweight paper for petals

HB pencil

Scissors, a normal pair and a pair of crimping craft scissors, optional

Invisible sticky tape

A variety of decorative punches — I used a small circle shape and a slightly smaller sun-shaped one

Small sheet 200gsm (approximately) patterned cardboard for discs for the centre of the flowers

Metal skewer and a block of old wood

Hammer or rubber mallet

12 or more silver brads

PVA glue

Acrylic paint and small paintbrush, optional

FOR EXTRA STRUCTURE

You may need extra wire if your lampshade does not have plenty of existing struts to attach the paper tape to. I had to add extra vertical lengths to make mine more stable and to make it easier to attach the flowers. The paper tape is very strong, especially when doubled over, so you might find you can get by without the wire additions, but if you need extra struts you will require:

Thinnish jewellery-making wire

Tin snips

Small craft pliers

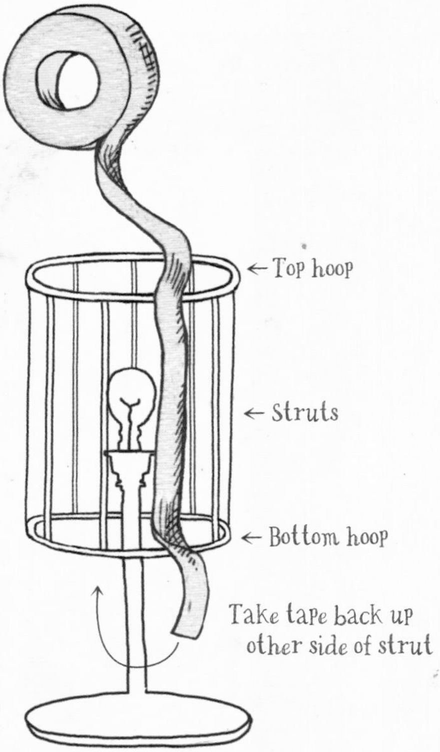

METHOD

1. Strip the lamp of all its original finery, leaving the basic wire structure and remove from lamp base.

2. If the existing wire struts are too widely spaced add some extra vertical wire struts using the jewellery-making wire. Ideally the struts should be about 10cm apart. Attach the extra struts neatly to the top and bottom hoops by crimping them with the pliers. These lengths of wire may slide around a bit but don't fret — the paper tape will sort that out.

3. Wind the brown paper tape around the top hoop. When you reach a strut, bring the tape down the outside of each strut, then under the bottom hoop and back up on the inside of the strut. Continue doing this until all the metal struts are covered with tape on the outside and inside. When you have finished covering the metal struts, there should be a few centimetres of space between the strips of tape. Finish covering any bare wire on the hoops by winding the tape around them. There should be no wire showing.

4. Transfer the flower templates, which are on the inside of the book's jacket, onto your card.

5. Fold 2–4 sheets of the brown paper, depending on the sharpness and accuracy of your scissors. Place the card template on the folded sheets, trace the outline onto the paper and cut out lots of petals. Use crimping craft scissors for some and plain scissors for the rest — this makes a nice variation. Continue until you have lots and lots of petals of varying sizes — the smaller ones will go on top of the bigger ones.

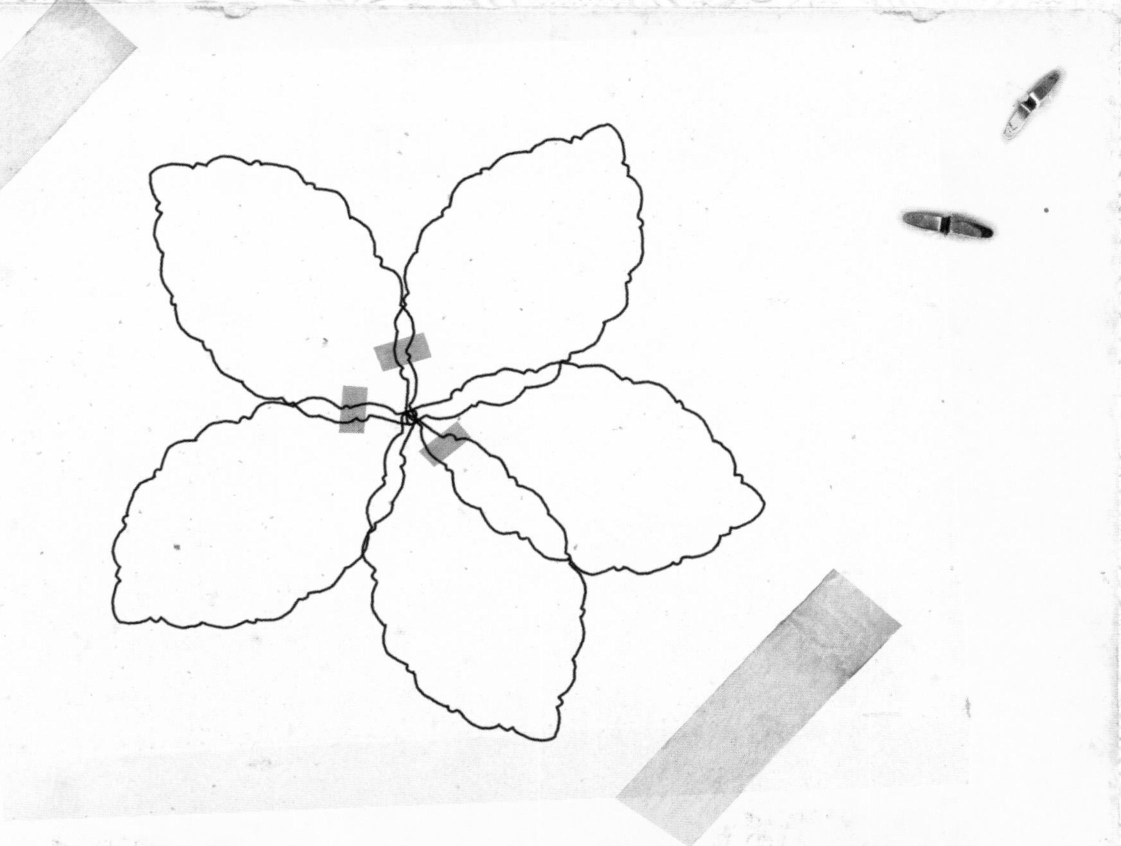

6. Arrange 5 of the largest petals in a circle slightly overlapping so they look like the outside petals of a flower (as shown above). Stick the petals to each other on the back with sticky tape, using as little tape as possible, otherwise it gets too bulky.

7. Repeat for the next layer of smaller petals. You will now have two layers of petals assembled. You can make three layers, if you like. Keep assembling flowers until you have enough to cover the lamp. I needed 20 to cover my frame, which was about 30cm tall.

8. Using a decorative craft punch, punch out your patterned paper discs for the centre of each flower. They should be about 4cm diameter.

9. Cut out the small discs from the 280gsm card to cover the back of each flower — this is where you will attach the flower to the paper tape. This makes them easier to attach to the lamp than if you simply tried to attach the brad to the brown paper tape.

10 Assemble the flowers by sandwiching the petal layers between the front and back discs. Place a completed flower on the block of wood and use the skewer and hammer or rubber mallet to drive a hole through the middle of the assembled flower. If it is too bulky to push the skewer through easily, do a layer at a time, but try to pierce the hole as close to the centre of each layer as possible.

11 Ease a brad through the hole, making the hole bigger if necessary. Fold back the metal prongs of the brad at the back of the flower. Turn the whole thing over and voila, you have a flower. Once you have made one, you will see if you need to adjust the position of the petals to make the whole thing symmetrical. Repeat with the remaining flowers.

12 Now start placing the flowers on the lamp. Place a small dab of PVA glue on the back of the flower and attach to the brown-paper tape. You may also need to use some extra brown-paper tape to secure them to the vertical struts. This will get very fiddly once you have a mass of flowers growing on your shade. You will have to come in from the top or bottom to attach the last few flowers. Do not fret about 'crushing' the petals — the kraft paper is surprisingly forgiving and in any case, I like this slightly crumpled look, as it adds to the whimsy and handmade feel of the piece. Keep going until you have covered enough of the surface to make it pleasing.

13 Add a long-life globe (compact fluorescent lamp) … and turn it on. The lamp looks lovely lit up and also au naturel, as I'm sure you will see.

WARNING If you use an incandescent globe make sure it is no more than 25 watts as, unlike the long-life globe, incandescent globes produce a lot of heat and can be a fire hazard if placed too close to paper.

IDEA

You can also paint the base and stem of the lamp. I used a flat oyster-hued acrylic to go over the original black base and was very pleased with the whole look.

Set a Mood

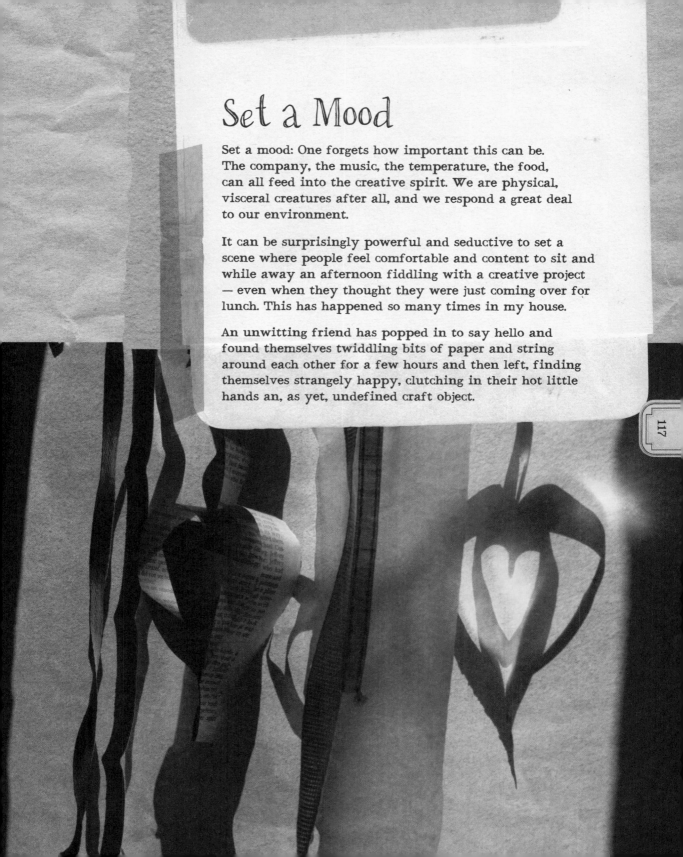

Set a mood: One forgets how important this can be. The company, the music, the temperature, the food, can all feed into the creative spirit. We are physical, visceral creatures after all, and we respond a great deal to our environment.

It can be surprisingly powerful and seductive to set a scene where people feel comfortable and content to sit and while away an afternoon fiddling with a creative project — even when they thought they were just coming over for lunch. This has happened so many times in my house.

An unwitting friend has popped in to say hello and found themselves twiddling bits of paper and string around each other for a few hours and then left, finding themselves strangely happy, clutching in their hot little hands an, as yet, undefined craft object.

VIA AIR MAIL
VIA AIR MAIL
JUN 8
1 30 PM
1935
UNITED STATES POSTAGE
6
6
BUY U.S. SAVINGS
BONDS
ASK YOUR POSTMASTER

Stamp Spotting

OK, OK, I know stamp collecting has had some bad press. But wow, what a lot I've discovered when investigating their uses for this book. Though I'm no stamp spotter — I'm not especially interested in their age, or where they're from, etc — I do find myself beguiled by their colour and design. That and the fact that so much is often packed into this little object that is just a couple of centimetres in size.

On opening a bag of random stamps attached to bits of torn envelopes that I bought from my local flea market recently, I found myself entranced by what spilled onto the table before me.

My urge was to group them by colour: I happily whiled away half an afternoon making little piles of stamp treasures, unsure of what I was going to do with them once sorted. I left them in their piles in a box for many months before revisiting them.

Determined to make some use of my stash, I took the whole lot with me in my suitcase to my mother's farm in Queensland. My partner's father was an old-school stamp collector, so it gave him some pleasure to see me fossicking about re-sorting the stamps into piles again when they'd become muddled from the trip. Ah, memories! My lad suggested I soak the stamps off the bits of torn envelopes, and dry them so I could see what I really had. It didn't take long: a big wide pan of very gently simmering water did the trick in no time at all. What fascinated me, however, was what was left behind once we'd pulled the stamps from the water. I was as attracted to the paper that had been attached to the backs of the stamps as much as I was to the pretty and colourful stamps themselves. Who'd have thought the insides of old envelopes held any design or craft possibilities?

What was lovely was that they were all made from thin paper, usually with a blue or grey pattern over the surface. When I turned them so that the patterned inside of each envelope showed, the resulting collage effect was very pleasing. I knew I had a few more projects I'd never have dreamed up otherwise right there!

ESPAÑA
Canada 78
CANADA
EIRE
NEDERLAND
25C
GULDEN
ÉIRE €1
PRIORITY
AUSTRALIA
malaysia
selangor
Canada 73
ÖSTERREICH
REPUBLIK ÖSTERREICH
REPUBLIK INDONESIA
30 sen
Polska
80zł
PAKISTAN
RSA
EUROPA
INTERNATIONAL WOMENS YEAR 1975
Suid-Afrika
South Africa
50c
NASIONALE SEëLDAG NATIONAL STAMP DAY
PILIPINAS
BUNDES
INDIA
PILGRIMS REST
20c
12C NEDERLAND
Republik Österreich

EASY

Stamp Artwork

I just love this project. It is easy and the results can be so varied. The collecting and sorting of old stamps is such fun. This is one of the few artworks I actually tried to plan, but having said that, in the end my instincts overtook me and I threw my plan to the wind. I was trying to use stamps of the same size to start with, and stamps in similar hues. But, in the end, randomness ruled! If you wish to make a plan, however, be my guest. Just expect it to change along the way!

YOU WILL NEED

Plywood board cut to the desired size of the artwork, I used 4 ply, approximately A3 in size

PVA glue

Paintbrush

Stamps (soaked off envelopes if necessary), sorted into colours and/or themes

Cling film

Brayer or rolling pin

Utility knife and cutting mat

Paint, optional

Picture hanger

METHOD

1. Start by sealing the plywood all over with PVA glue diluted with 50% water. Let this dry.

2. Place some undiluted PVA glue in a bowl and lightly paint it onto a strip of the board, starting at one corner. Don't cover the whole board, only paint a small section.

3. Start sticking down your stamps, following your plan (if you have one). As the PVA glue dries, brush a little more onto the surface of the board and continue gluing down the stamps. It doesn't matter too much if you dab some glue onto the stamps, as PVA glue dries clear. Keep going until you reach an edge, then turn around and start back. Continue zigzagging until you have finished the whole board. Do not worry about stamps hanging over the edge as you will cut them off when the glue is dry.

4. Stretch a layer of cling film over the board to prevent gluey bits sticking to the roller. Gently roll with the brayer or rolling pin until the stamps are very flat without any air bubbles or grit. Once the stamps are totally flat, peel off the cling film before it sticks to the stamps. Another method is to lay the cling film over the artwork once it has dried a bit and then put the whole lot under a pile of heavy books for the night.

5. When the artwork is bone dry, turn it upside down and carefully slice the overhanging edges off, using the edge of the plywood as a guide.

6. If you want to, paint the visible edges of ply with paint – gold paint or gold or silver leaf looks especially good.

7. Paint the entire surface and edges with one coat of fairly thick PVA glue, or paint on several lighter layers. Let it dry.

8. Attach the picture hanger to the back, hang up your masterpiece and marvel.

IDEA

You could tea-stain the whole affair after you've glued everything down. When it has dried, varnish it.

TO TEA-STAIN

I simply make a cup of tea with a teabag, and then squeeze out the bag until it is almost dry. Rub this over the surface of the artwork, and it will leave a pleasant, instant, aged effect in its wake. You may need to use more than one teabag if the first dries out too quickly. My teabags usually break in the process ... but don't fret if this happens to you too, the offending tea leaves brush off when dried.

31P
15½P
37P
EMBE
e the
COD
8P
POSTAGE
HONG KONG
2P

3c
AUSTRALIA
HONGKONG $1
HONG KONG
12p
18p
30p
22p
4c
AUSTRALIA
4c
AUSTRALIA
35p

EASY

Riveting Trivet

This is a modern take on the old method of decoupage using the random bits of envelopes you were maybe going to discard in the Stamp Artwork project (see page 120). It is easy as you don't have to be too thoughtful about colour since there are really only two colours, grey and blue. If 'more is more' is my usual motto, then in this case 'less is more'! You're forced into a sober palette by the subdued designs inside most envelopes.

If you haven't got the discarded envelopes from Stamp Artwork, then just a few days worth of mail is really all you need in order to have a variety of paper. Be sure to keep any airmail envelopes as they make for interesting bursts of red and some arresting diagonal stripes.

YOU WILL NEED

Lots of pieces of torn envelopes

Plywood cut to desired size of the artwork, I used 4 ply, approximately A3 in size

PVA glue

Disposable paintbrush

Cling film

Brayer or rolling pin

METHOD

1. Arrange torn pieces of envelopes so any designs are facing up.

2. Seal the plywood with PVA glue diluted with 50% water. Let this dry.

3. Place some undiluted PVA glue in a bowl and lightly paint it onto a strip of the board, starting at one corner. Don't cover the whole board. Do a small section at a time.

4. Start sticking down your envelope pieces to the PVA glue strip straight away as the PVA glue dries very quickly. This is a little freer than the Stamp Artwork project because you can tear each piece into whatever size you like since you aren't limited by the size of the actual stamp. (You can always add extra bits or strips to cover bare patches after the main surface has been covered, so don't fret.)

5. Stretch a layer of cling film over the board to prevent gluey bits sticking to the roller and gently roll the envelope pieces with a brayer or rolling pin until they are very flat, without any air bubbles. Once they are totally flat, peel off the cling wrap before it sticks to the paper. Another method to remove wrinkles and bubbles is to lay the cling wrap over the artwork once it has dried a bit and then put it under a pile of heavy books overnight.

6. When everything is bone dry, paint the entire surface and the edges with one coat of undiluted PVA glue, or paint on several lighter layers. Let it dry for a few days before using.

W. A. & Sons (N) Ltd.
OUTWARD
70115
70116
70117
70118

The Art of Mess

I have made many serendipitous artistic discoveries by — I hate to admit it — having a whole lot of mess on the table. If you asked my dear mother, she'd say that this sounds like a justification for the debris that was usually left in my wake throughout my childhood. Alas, it has taken me half a lifetime to realise that there is value in a jumble of buttons, ribbons, envelopes, books, papers, boxes and paper bags — they can reveal a marriage of colour, texture or form that I would never have deliberately put together.

Sifting can be quite a gift. Stumbling upon things I hadn't even realised were there has been the foundation of many a productive afternoon, the start of a great new range of ideas. In mess I can find the perfectly satisfying conclusion to a design or project that seemed to need just that extra bit of pattern or texture or colour. And sometimes it can seem frustratingly obvious: *why didn't I think of that before?*

The truth is that for those like me, mess is beauty, mess is pleasure.

Consciously arranging things is not the only way of making art. A bit of unself-conscious mess can lead to unexpected discoveries, or, if you like, 'divine inspiration'. Just don't tell your mother that! She will probably never believe you.

whatever you do, don't panic

TEMPLATE PROVIDED

EASY

Paper Dolly

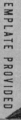

It must be a hangover from childhood, but I love a paper doll. There are so many ways to change their looks and personalities. I have a great book I picked up in the Bethnal Green Museum of Childhood in London called Dean's Rag Books and Rag Dolls *by Peter and Dawn Cope that I dip into for inspiration. Have fun with this simple project — it really only requires some simple cutting.*

YOU WILL NEED

280gsm A4 card, or larger, depending on the size of your doll

Glue stick

Utility knife and cutting mat, or scissors

Scrap patterned paper

Ribbon, optional

Brad, optional

METHOD

1. Photocopy the template above. You can enlarge her to any size you like.

2. Using your glue stick, glue the photocopied girl onto your card. If you are using my clothing and shoes, do the same with these also. Each piece of clothing has its own tabs so you can attach the clothing to the doll's body.

3. Using the knife and mat, or scissors, cut out your doll.

4. If you want to attach a ribbon around the doll's middle (as seen on following page), simply cut a length of ribbon and put a brad through it to hold it in place.

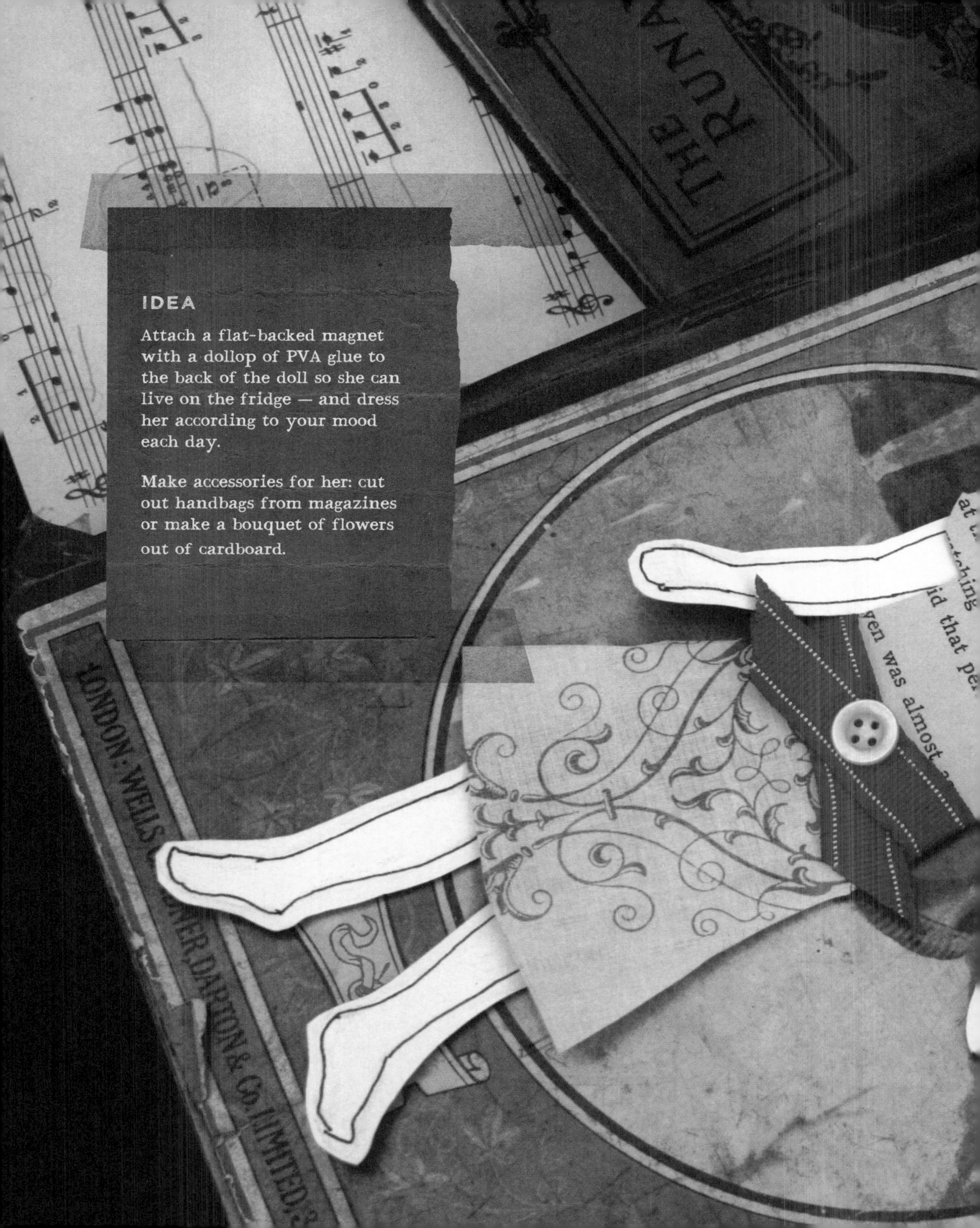

IDEA

Attach a flat-backed magnet with a dollop of PVA glue to the back of the doll so she can live on the fridge — and dress her according to your mood each day.

Make accessories for her: cut out handbags from magazines or make a bouquet of flowers out of cardboard.

LYRA FARB-RIESE - COLOR-GIANT 93027
GERMANY
LYRA 93061
BOX.
Xx

Creativity comes from trust.
Trust your instincts.

RITA MAE BROWN

love

Some friends and I sat around on my mum's farm one steamy March afternoon and cottoned on to the fact that there was some very posh 4-ply paper sitting in the loo. So after tearing leaves of tissue off into separate sheets, one of us took to them with scissors, creating the rough circles for the petals, and someone else made a pink wash from watercolour paints. Holding them in a stack, we stained the edges of the circles and waved them about the place to dry.

Excellent! After a glass or two of champagne, we had assembled some lovely, interesting and very soft flowers. Then one of our number made stamens by twisting small lengths of paper into straws, which she then tied around each other. Someone else interleaved a few rounds of thinner ply toilet paper, which resulted in a pleasing textural and colour change among the petals.

All of these layers were then secured with a brad and a small firm cardboard disc at the back for ballast and easy attaching. Even the lads were impressed — in a smirky kind of way — with our ingenuity.

EASY

Paper Roses

You can make these wonderful, ephemeral roses out of any thin kind of paper. We just chose to be irreverent and used toilet paper for those pictured here. (See the photo of some made from patterned text-weight paper on pages 142–143). You can alter and have fun with them in a myriad of ways: try slotting some contrasting coloured tissue paper in between a few leaves of the toilet paper. Or make a short fringe from some sheet music and secure it in the centre of the flower with the brad.

YOU WILL NEED

Patterned or plain 80gsm paper or thick toilet paper

Small piece of 280gsm card

Good sharp scissors

Small disposable paintbrush, optional

Watercolour paints, optional

Sharp pointed scalpel or metal skewer and a block of old wood

Brads

METHOD

1. Cut circles out of the paper of the diameter you want the finished flower to be. Ours were about 9cm.

2. If you want to tint the edges of the petals, dip your paintbrush in water, load it with the watercolour paint of your choice and gently paint the edges of the paper. Let the petals dry.

3. Cut a small circular disc (about 3cm) from the card to attach to the underside of the rose. This makes it easier to hang or pin.

4. Pierce a hole through the centre of the stack of petals, large enough for the 'legs' of the brad to go through with ease. We used a combination of a metal skewer and a sharp scalpel blade. Don't make it so big that the head of the brad will also slip through. Pierce all the layers, including the disc.

5. Thread the brad through the layers. Fold back the prongs of the brad to secure. It should be looking very much like a flower now.

6. Scrunch up the top few layers of the flower. Don't be afraid! We were a little timid to start with but soon went to it with gusto. In any case, we fancy that the creases, even when apparently 'accidents', add character. Primp and fashion the top half of the 'flower' until you are happy with it.

IDEAS

If you fancy it, make some 'leaves' and place them on the underside of the flower before you place the round disc in position, then pierce through all the layers, including the leaves with a skewer and put the brad through.

Make some stamens by rolling lengths of thin paper or toilet paper into sausage shapes and securing them under the brad when you push it through. Be aware that the coiled up tissue might get a bit bulky so try to keep the middle bit of each stamen flattish.

Make a Christmas wreath of 25 or so of these. It might sound like a lot but they are so easy and, once you get into a rhythm, they're quite addictive! Make a simple armature from metal coathangers or nicely-shaped twigs and sticks. If using coathangers, cover the wire with long strips of newspaper, wrapping it around several times to hide the wire. Attach the flowers randomly around the armature, perhaps adding some extra leaves if you wish. You can stain the leaves a deep red or green with watercolours, or use red or green paper. Soon you will have a very cheap, very effective and very lovely homemade wreath!

Of course you can use decorative paper instead of toilet paper as the example on the next page shows.

CHATTERBOX

HARD

Vintage Journal

I just love this idea. Take one of those old-fashioned kid's annuals with a cloth spine and transform it into a new journal for your own thoughts and musings using what is called 'Japanese binding'. You can achieve so many different textures and effects by using old book covers to fashion 'new' journals.

As this project involves drilling and some quite fine finger work with the sewing of the spine, it is best left to the oldies.

YOU WILL NEED

Thick old-fashioned kid's annual — it must have a cloth spine that is no less than 15cm wide

Enough sheets of 80gsm blank paper to be half the thickness of the original book, cut 15mm wider than the original cover of the book to allow for the stitching

2 pieces of scrap wood the same dimensions as the journal

2 clamps

Drill with a 3mm diameter drill bit

Carpet or sail maker's needle

String or nylon twine

PVA glue, optional

METHOD

1. Remove the original pages from the old book. Keep these pages for other projects: they are a great resource. Neatly stack your new journal pages.

2. Tightly wrap the old book cover around your journal pages. Make sure the pages are hard up against the back of the old cloth spine and that the cloth spine wraps around at least 15mm on the front and back. Everything should be absolutely square. Clamp the book between the two pieces of wood. The wood must align with the spine. The wood and clamping will stop any movement while you drill and also prevent any ripping of the paper.

3. Mark the positions of the holes on the wood 10mm from the spine. The first and last holes need to be 5mm from each end of the book, then space each hole in between about 20mm apart.

IMPORTANT The holes should pass through the cloth spine of the old cover, not through the boards of the cover. If they don't pass through both sides of the cloth, you will need to adjust by reducing the number of journal pages.

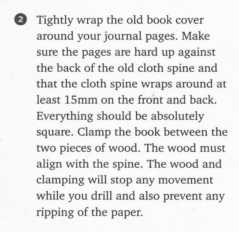

4. Drill your holes through the wood, cloth and book pages. Once drilled, discard the wood.

5. If your book is old and a bit fragile as mine was, reinforce the cloth spine on the inside with fabric or brown-paper tape before stitching it all together.

6. With a needle and heavy thread or twine, start at one end of the spine and blanket stitch through the predrilled holes until you reach the other end. Then blanket stitch back again from the other side. You will end up with a double thickness of stitching, which tends to look better and holds the pages more snugly. Tie the two ends of thread together in a neat, small knot. Although not necessary, a small spot of PVA glue will also help to keep this from unravelling.

7. Make a cup of tea and start to think about what you are going to write or draw in your journal.

IDEA

Add interest to the journal pages by stamping some of them with a rubber stamp that reflects your theme, or use some of the pages for collages while leaving the others blank for writing on.

The Joy of Old Books

I collect paper like my father collected records. I covet different textures as though I'm a bowerbird: one day it's torn and aged sheets of music, the next it's cheap paperbacks or fabric-bound hardcovers. Both my partner and I have a thing for the smell of old paper. We sneak our noses into the pages of aged books and sniff, and fancy we are drawing in the history. I find much to inspire me in the pages of old books: I love the marks that the weather and use has made; and I love the old typefaces, the way they subtly bleed into the thick, yellowing fibres of the paper.

And while I am loath to rip up gorgeous old books for art and craft projects, I occasionally do so. I try not to start reading them, so as not to get involved, mad as that may seem. It's better if we haven't had a relationship, if you know what I mean.

It can be enormous fun just sitting about cutting out random words, headings or sentences from old books with a small, sharp pair of scissors, and assembling them onto another sheet of paper — the yellower and mustier the better. Recently a family friend and I were thinking of a person we both knew and started to write 'poetry' about them in this way. Sticking down the random words resulted in a nonsense poem that was quite strikingly accurate and certainly interesting. Much laughter ensued. Such happy accidents are all part of the fun of paper crafting.

SHAFT TAIL FINCH
POLSKA
NEW SOUTH WALES POSTAGE
EXERCISE
Simplicity
5323
ONE SIZE
APPLICATION
BRA FINCH

EASY

Rustic Object Rubbings

This is a lovely way for kids to begin to understand texture and form. You might find you go a bit nuts after doing a few of these rubbings and want to 'rub' over all manner of odd things!

YOU WILL NEED

Variety of soft pencils: HB, 2B, 3B and/or a selection of soft coloured pencils or crayons

Variety of objects that have a relief pattern — coins, for example

80gsm printing paper, A4 coloured or plain paper

METHOD

1. Place your paper over the relief pattern. Gently rub your pencil or crayon over the entire pattern until you start to see the impression come through. Keep going until you have a density of colour that you are happy with. (The good thing is that if you tear a few sheets of paper, there's no great loss, you can always start another one.)

2. When you have amassed a few rubbings, choose your favourites, mount them and frame them, or make cards out of them.

IDEA

Move the humble coin-rubbing scenario up a notch and rub objects in your neighbourhood that have an embossed pattern, like signs or plaques, headstones in an historic cemetery ... or whatever takes your fancy. If you feel a little self-conscious doing this, just say you're engaged in some guerrilla art tactics!

EASY

Articulated Girl

This project is unlike me in many ways: she's plain and unadorned. She's just nice, bright and white. She's vaguely modelled on some puppets I bought in Indonesia ... I liked the idea that she could bend and move a bit and the brads make her quite interactive. The options, of course, are endless: you could paint her, cover her in the pages of an old book, decoupage her, dress her in so many ways. You could even make a mate for her by adjusting the shapes a bit to become more masculine. But I quite like her as she is: part mermaid, tossed about on the sea of life.

YOU WILL NEED

280gsm or heavier card, standard box cartons are ideal

Utility knife and cutting mat for adults and small sharp scissors for kids

Coloured images cut from lightweight card, less than 280gsm, so the limbs aren't too raised and bulky from the side, optional

Glue stick or PVA glue, optional

Brayer or rolling pin, optional

Metal skewer and a piece of old wood

Brads

Fishing line, optional

TEMPLATE PROVIDED

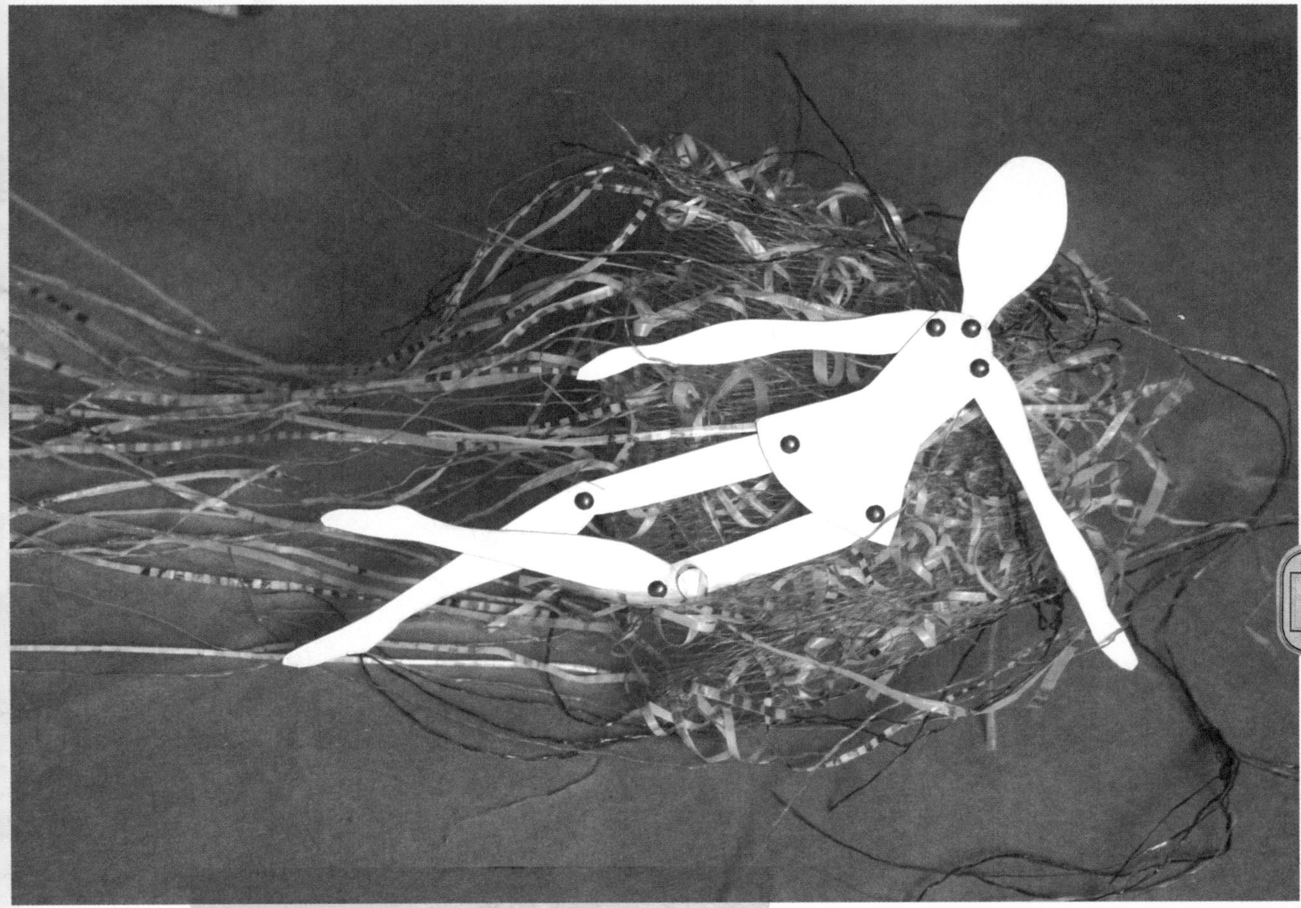

String vessel by Annie Aitken

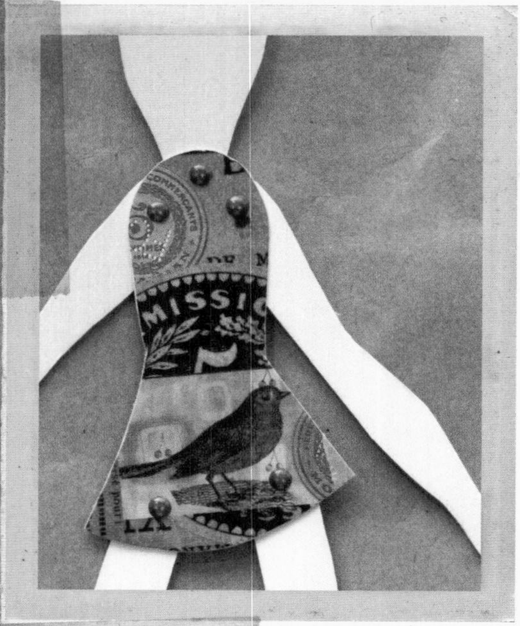

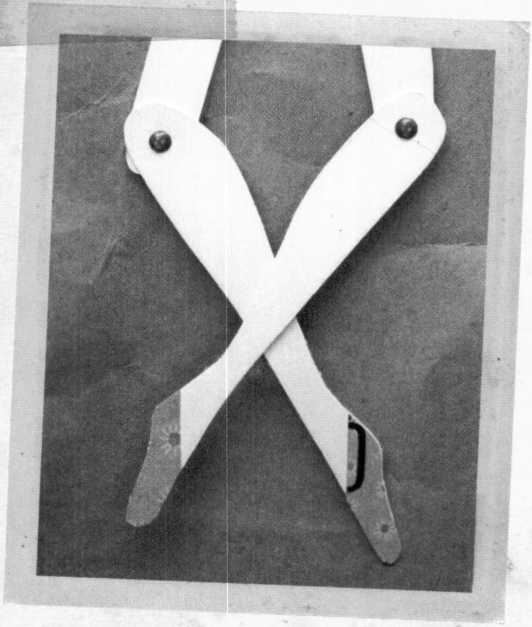

METHOD

1. Transfer the template, which is on the inside of the book's jacket, onto your card.

2. Cut out the body shapes with your knife or with sharp scissors. (Don't let children use the utility knife, it is way too scary.)

3. If you want your articulated girl to be covered with patterned paper or the pages of an old book, glue the paper to the front and back of the body parts. Using a brayer, roll over the paper to get rid of any wrinkles, and leave to dry before assembling.

4. Assemble the body pieces, and place on the block of wood. With the metal skewer, make a hole where the brads will go. Attach the head and limbs to the girl's body using the brads. Now you have an articulated girl that can lie about and look lovely, or simply punch a small hole through the top of her head, thread through some fine fishing line and dangle her from a shelf, or another spot in the house.

Paste
POST
15cm角
10柄
10枚入

Paper Exercise

Gather together a few of your favourite papers and some bits and pieces.

You may already have a box with favourite finds in it.

See how many ways you can join paper to an object.

See if they make a story. Staple, sew or stick your papers together with glue, washi tape, masking tape or brown-paper tape.

Affix them with thumbtacks, paper fasteners, paperclips. Punch holes through them and tie with string or ribbon.

Peg them together.

Play with the layers and with the opacity of the papers.

Squint your eyes at them and start to see tonal similarities or patterns emerging.

Gather them thematically this way.

Have lots of fun!

THE RUN
THE RUN
WAYS

GRAVOX
OXO

EASY

Decoupage Drawers

My partner came up with this project. Fond as he is of antique and vintage things, he put some newspapers that he had found under his floorboards to good use with the help of his kids. It just takes time and a bit of patience.

YOU WILL NEED

Old newspapers

Scissors

Wallpaper paste, mixed to a yoghurt consistency

Old chest of drawers that needs an overhaul

Large clean sponge, lightly dampened

Acrylic varnish to finish

Teabag for tea-staining, optional

METHOD

1. Choose your newspapers then roughly cut them into pieces no larger than A4 — any larger makes them hard to handle and smooth down. Try to find interesting advertisements or logos and headlines to feature.

2. Cover your floor with extra newspaper (this is a messy project) and prepare your wallpaper paste. Remove the drawers from the chest and set aside.

3. Paint the wallpaper paste onto one side of the newspaper and start laying it down on the chest. Beginning at a corner or edge is always good. Smooth down the pieces of paper as you go, using your hands or an ever so slightly damp sponge. Keep going until you reach a corner, overlapping and playing with the design as you go. (You can always paper over anything you don't like, so don't worry too much.)

4. Carefully take the pieces of paper over all the edges and curves that will be visible, smoothing them down as you go to remove any air bubbles. When you come to a drawer cavity, continue the paper around the lip for about 10cm so that when you open the drawers you will see the pattern inside. Leave the chest to dry.

5. Now start on the drawers. Have some fun with the way you lay down the paper or where you place the advertisements. You could even cut out letters and make words pertaining to the owner of the drawers.

6. Wait until everything is completely dry (some days preferably), then coat the chest of drawers with acrylic varnish to protect it. You could even add some new knobs or feet as we did. When totally dry, insert the drawers.

7. If you want an old faded look, tea-stain the entire chest of drawers before you vanish it. See page 123 for tea-staining instructions.

POST-CARD
www.skyesthelimit.com.au
POST CARD
Royal Flying Corps
said Alice.
the Pigeon. "I can see you
lice, rather doubtfully,
ages she had gone
Pigeon in a
value no ones judgm
{ love }
www.skyesthelimit.com.au

PACKAGING

There is nothing quite like making a complete present of your craft project. Packaging can make all the difference.

Find small boxes you can alter, or make your own from scratch. I often paper over matchboxes or the boxes teabags come in to make a snug home for a craft present.

Shredded newspaper or wood wool makes a lovely bed for your craft project.

EASY

Paper-cobbled Coasters

These look amazing and were dreamed up by my partner's sister, Jenny. She is very creative … and obviously patient because while this is not a complicated project, it does take time and patience. I actually think they're too lovely to use as coasters, so I display mine on the wall.

YOU WILL NEED

2 sheets of crepe paper, each of a different colour

Scissors

2 bowls to hold the crepe balls

Cork coasters (available from craft supply stores)

Black felt-tip pen

PVA glue

Small flattish bowl for glue

L O
V E

METHOD

1. Neatly fold over the crepe paper of one colour several times so it is no wider than 4cm, then cut it into 7cm strips. Having all the strips the same size is the key to a nice, smooth, flattish surface. Repeat the process for the second colour.

2. Screw up each strip into a little ball, rolling it with your hands as though you're rolling pasta or making meatballs. Place each set of coloured balls into its own bowl.

3. Using a felt-tip pen, draw your design onto the cork coasters. The design can be as simple as a star or a number or letters that spell out a word when put together. Random patterns are nice too, but don't make them too complicated.

4. Place the PVA glue into the small flat bowl. Apply PVA glue to a small section of the cork surface.

5. Start sticking down the tightly rolled crepe balls of the first colour, adding a dab of PVA glue to the bottom of each crepe ball before putting it into place.

6. Keep going with each coaster until you have completed the first colour, then start on the second. The good thing is, you can always play with the design a little while the glue is drying, easing the paper off the cork and replacing it if necessary.

7. When you are finished, let it completely dry and then to protect it, cover it with another layer of PVA glue which will dry clear.

IDEA

Become adventurous and try more than two colours. You could use the third colour sparingly and just for highlights, perhaps.

Curiosity about life in all of its aspects, I think, is still the secret of great creative people.

LEO BURNETT

174

MODERATE

Paper Bird Brooch

Because it is great fun working out combinations of different birds, you will probably end up making a few. This project calls for a bit of precision if your birds are to look great, so take your time.

YOU WILL NEED

Pieces of 280gsm card in various colours and patterns

Utility knife and cutting mat for adults and small sharp scissors for kids

Light sandpaper or a sanding block

PVA glue or glue stick

Pointy tweezers

Brooch fastener or magnet attachment

Button

Thread

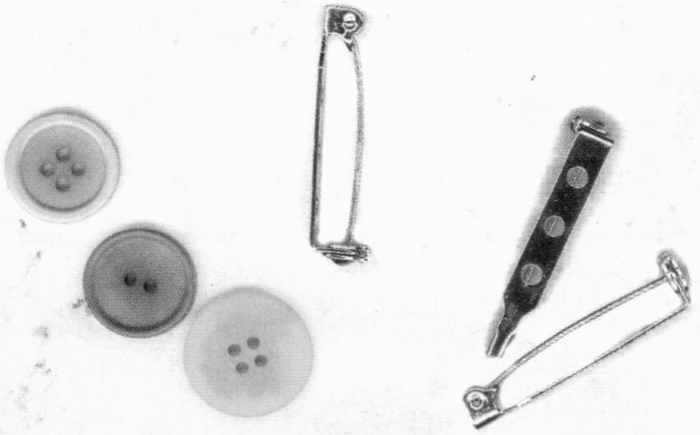

175
TEMPLATE PROVIDED

METHOD

1. Transfer the template, which is on the inside of the book's jacket, onto your card.

2. Carefully cut out the different pieces from the card using your utility knife or scissors. Use a small sanding block or a piece of sandpaper wrapped around a matchbox to tidy up any daggy edges — remember we want neatness with this one folks!

3. Before gluing the pieces into place, make sure you are clear about the order in which to glue them down. Use full-strength PVA glue or a good quality glue stick. Let the bottom layers dry before placing the upper layers, so there is less chance of the pieces moving about. If you are having difficulty, use tweezers to help you place the pieces on top of one another.

4. Start by gluing piece 2 to the base piece 1. Now glue the long tail feathers (3, 4 and 5) in place followed by the shorter tail feathers (6, 7 and 8) on top. Complete the feathers by placing the wing (9) on top. Finally, glue the beak (10) into position

5. Carefully press all the pieces firmly down by rolling a brayer over them, or put cling film over the bird and place under a pile of heavy books overnight.

6. When the bird is completely dry, complete its eye by stitching the button into place using colourful thread.

7. Attach magnets or brooch fasteners to the back of the bird with PVA glue. Finito!

AN OWL ALTERNATIVE

1. As for the small bird, transfer the owl template from the inside of the book's jacket onto your card, and then follow the Steps 2 and 3. Replace Step 4 with:

2. Start by gluing piece 2 to the base piece 1, then place the wings (3 and 4) into position. Add the beak (5) and the two eyeballs (6) and pupils (7). Finally to the back of piece 1, glue in place the two legs (8).

3. Now complete your owl by following Steps 5 and 7.

IDEAS

For the small bird, add embellishments such as 'jewels' or red feathers.

For the owl, cut out the two sets of wings so he has his full complement of wings showing.

TUCK'S POST CARD
POST CARD

POSTCARD
Raphael Tuck & Sons "OILETTE"
FAVOURITE FLOWERS
1. A Savings Bank may be established in connection with any P
or department, and the principal Teacher of such school, or depa
act as the Manager of the Bank.
2. Deposits of one penny and upwards (but not including an odd
will be received at the School, from enrolled pupils, any Monday, f
till o'clock.
3. Every deposit received by the Manager of a School Bank will
by him at the time, in a numbered book, and such entry will be
him; and the said book, with the entry so attested, will be g
depositor, and retained by him as evidence of the receipt of the de
his name and write his address in the places p
will be paid by him int
vings Bank, to the cr
of the Unde
s truste
overnme Savings
shier, with the usual
k in Sydn to the c
etary.
of their de
to be in a for
time, the deposit
aches one poun
d to open
and he
to th
acce
acc
tru
at the
continue to pay into the School Bank a
furnished with deposit Bo
charge; but, should it be lost he will be charged for a new
8. Repayments will be made only to the person, or to
of an order under his hand in case a
School Bank, such mone
relatives or guardian
Instruction entitled to receiv
45 Lon

I have destroyed a fair few of these little portable art boxes over the years. While buying myself one for my art materials, I realised that if I removed the hinges I would have two great little natural looking shadow boxes. And so that is what I did, and began putting little treasures inside the boxes' compartments. Soon I had a whole parade — some with hand made dolls in them — and quite a few colour-themed varieties too. I ended up going to the market to sell many of them, as it was getting a bit silly keeping them all to myself.

MODERATE

Shadow Box of Treasures

YOU WILL NEED

Artist's wooden materials box, hinges taken off so that you have two 'shadow boxes'

Manila luggage tags (from stationery suppliers or art stores), or make your own from cutting up manila folders and punching a hole through the top

Felt-tip black pen

Watercolour paints

Paintbrush

Little pegs, 4–5cm long

Utility knife and cutting mat for adults and small sharp scissors for kids

Metal ruler

Heavyweight card (280gsm or heavier)

Small piece of brown kraft paper (or use an old-fashioned lunchbag)

Rubber stamp with an image to match your theme

PVA glue

Brayer or rolling pin

Pages from an old dictionary or book

Set square, optional

Disposable paintbrush

8–10 small balsa wood pieces (available from craft shops) slightly less wide than the compartments you will be placing them in

Words, letters and images cut from magazines

Picture hanger for the back

METHOD

1. Place your shadow box in front of you and work out where you want to place your precious additions and what sort of theme you want to create — organic and natural or funky and colourful, fantasy and otherworldly or a return to childhood — it's up to you. Here, I've chosen a more muted, natural theme as you can see from the photo on page 180.

2. First check the size of your manila tags against the box and cut them to size if they are too big. Draw on the manila tags with your black felt-tip pen anything that takes your fancy and that fits into your theme. If you are not confident with drawing, stick images from cards or magazines on the tags instead. The good thing is, if you've bought quite a few tags (they are usually sold in bundles), you can keep trying until you're happy with your design.

3. Use watercolours to paint some areas of the tags. Let them dry and then attach the small pegs to the holes.

4. To line the back of the middle compartment with a page from a dictionary or book, first measure the size and then, using a metal ruler, cut the paper with your utility knife on the cutting mat (you may even want to use a set square as a guide). Apply an even layer of PVA glue to the back of the paper with the disposable paintbrush and glue the piece of paper down into place, taking care to push it gently into the corners of the box. If it is too wide, trim with good sharp scissors.

5. Using the cutting mat, utility knife and metal ruler as a guide, cut a rectangle or square of card that is a few centimetres smaller than the middle compartment. Cut a piece of brown kraft paper that is a few centimetres larger all round than the piece of card. Stamp the paper with the image you've chosen. Using PVA glue, mount the image on the card. Use the brayer to flatten it and to get rid of any air bubbles. Fold any excess paper to the back, mitre the corners and glue down. So the card doesn't get lost at the back of the compartment, use a block of balsa wood as a prop for the card and glue it to the back of the compartment, then glue the stamped image to the prop.

6. Select words, sentences and images you like, and stick them onto small balsa wood blocks using PVA glue. Use the brayer to flatten and firmly secure them.

7. Place the covered balsa wood blocks at the front of the bottom compartment, then attach the blocks to the base with PVA glue.

8. Fit your manila tags into the top compartment using PVA glue. (Once again use balsa wood props if necessary to bring the tags towards the front.)

9. As you can see I've kept my box 'raw' because I like the look, but you might want to use diluted PVA glue to seal and protect it. When you're done, attach a picture hanger to the back, and hang it up.

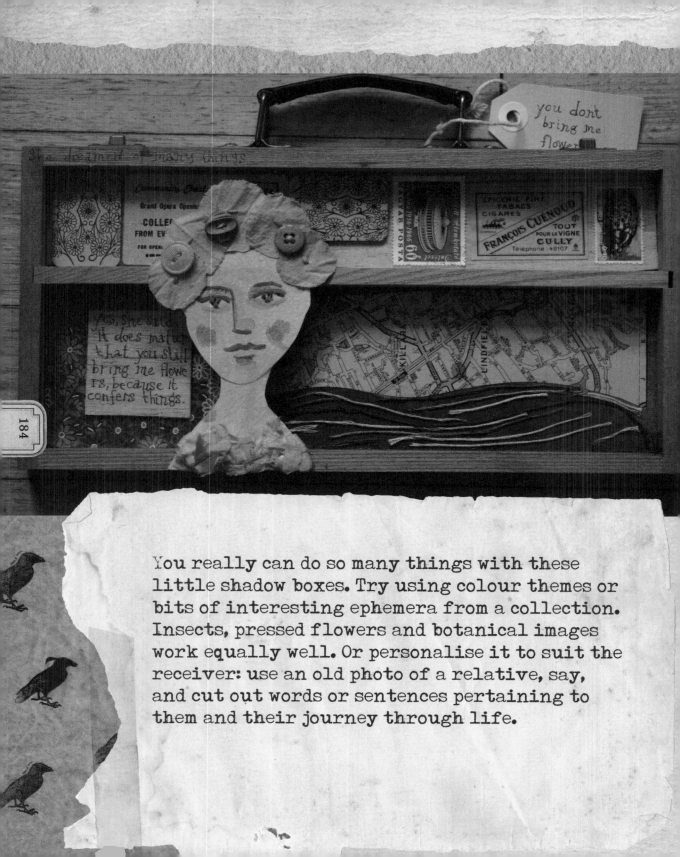

You really can do so many things with these little shadow boxes. Try using colour themes or bits of interesting ephemera from a collection. Insects, pressed flowers and botanical images work equally well. Or personalise it to suit the receiver: use an old photo of a relative, say, and cut out words or sentences pertaining to them and their journey through life.

MAKE YOUR OWN SHADOW BOX

You could always make your own shadow box out of balsa wood. You can buy balsa wood in a variety of lengths and widths from hobby or craft stores or online.

Make the shadow box as small or as large as you wish. To assemble it is easy, simply glue the strips of balsa wood onto a backing board with balsa wood glue. Firmly hold or clamp the pieces together for a few minutes or until they are adhered.

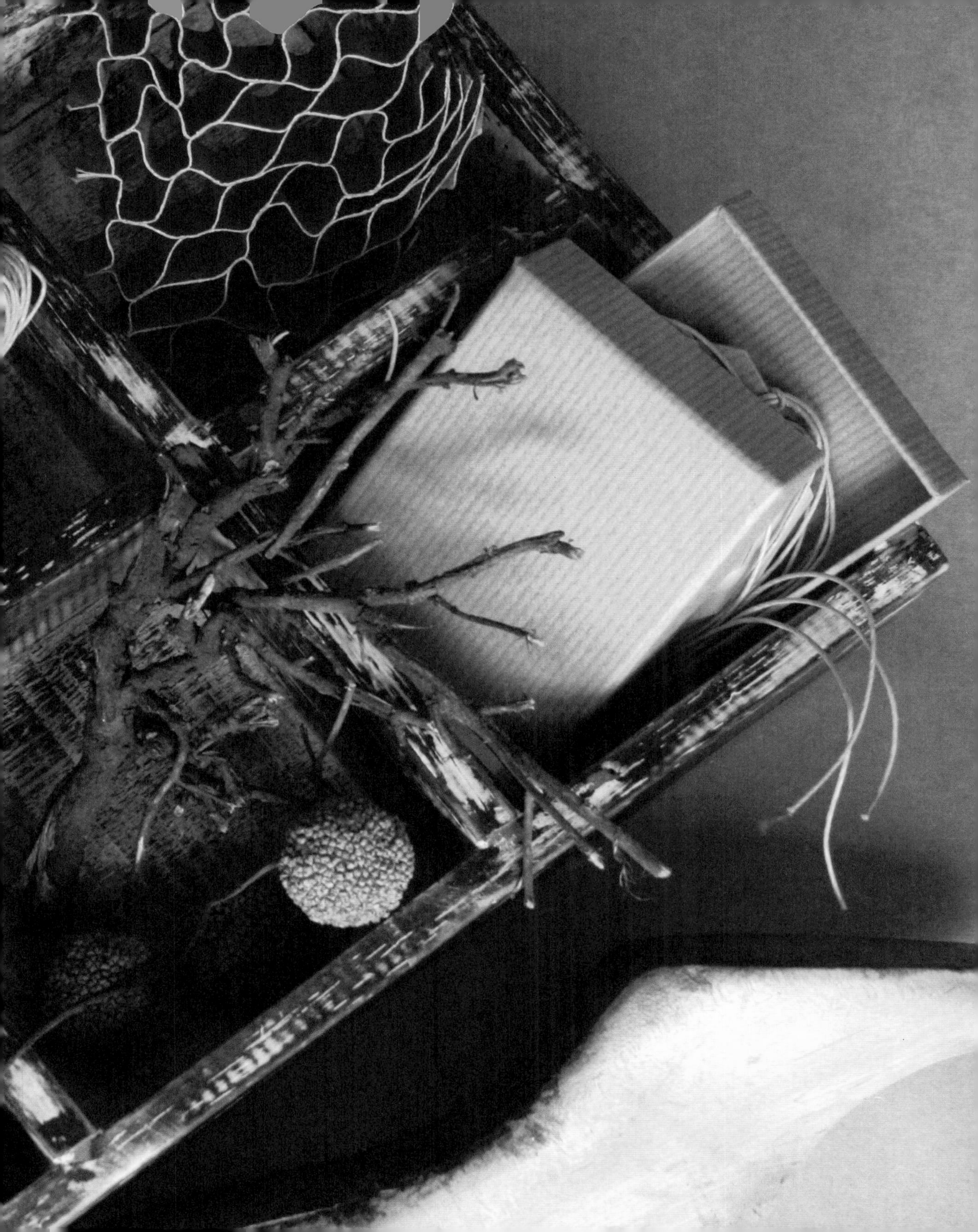

HARD

Slinky Snake Toy

The amazing thing about this terrific snake is that it really slithers — as long as the surface it is rolling on is smooth and even. It is one of the trickier projects but with patience and precision, especially with the folding of the pleated paper body, you will produce a wonderful object that will give pleasure to children and adults alike.

YOU WILL NEED

Plasticine

Newspaper, ripped into 3–4cm squares for the papier-mâché head

Wallpaper paste, mixed to a yoghurt consistency

Metal ruler

Utility knife and cutting mat

Sheet of text-weight paper 70cm long (wrapping paper is good) for the snake body

A weighty wooden cotton reel through which you can drill an extra hole, or a 3.5cm length of wooden broom handle (or something of a similar girth that has a bit of weight) through which two holes can be drilled

Drill or metal skewer

Plain of decorative paper for the head

Approximately 8cm of rubber band (cut an 8cm rubber band so it becomes a strip)

1.5m of fine string

A thin piece of dowel 5cm long x 1cm diameter, approximately, or a stick of similar length (as we have used here)

PVA glue

Buttons

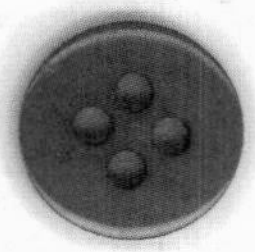

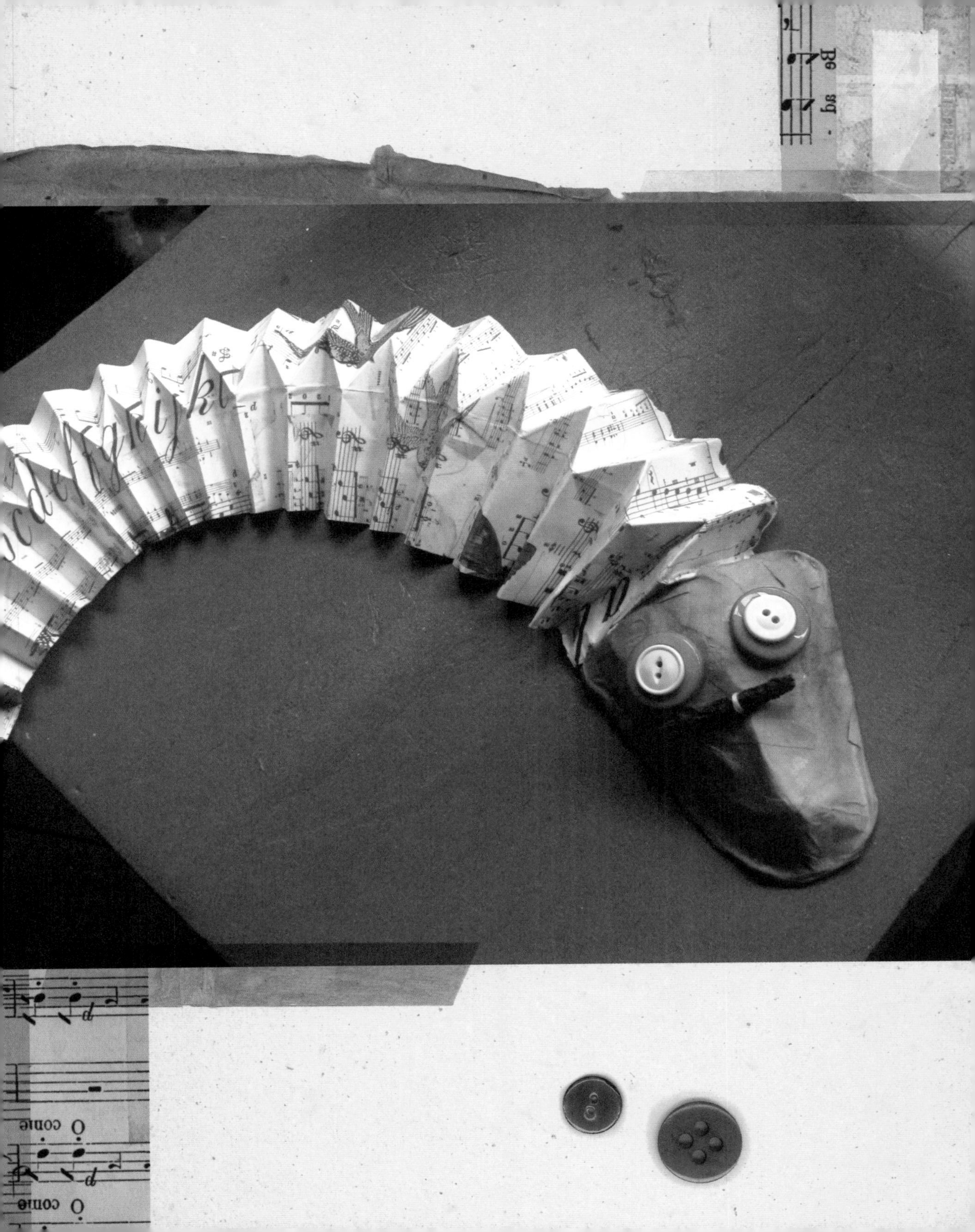

METHOD

1. First make the snake's head. Fashion a handful of plasticine into a wedge shape to make the head. It should be approximately 9cm at its widest point and 12cm long. It must be wide and high enough to easily accommodate the wooden cotton reel.

2. Using the plasticine snake head as a mould, make a papier-mâché head with the newspaper dipped in the wallpaper paste. Do at least a dozen layers of paper to give the head strength. Let it dry thoroughly.

3. When dry, ease the papier-mâché head off the plasticine mould. Trim it with scissors if there are some daggy bits.

4. While the head is drying, fashion the snake's body. Using your metal ruler, utility knife and cutting mat, cut a wedge-shaped rectangle from the paper, making the widest end slightly wider than the base of the papier-mâché head (approximately 10cm) and the tail end approximately 7.5cm wide (see Diagram 1).

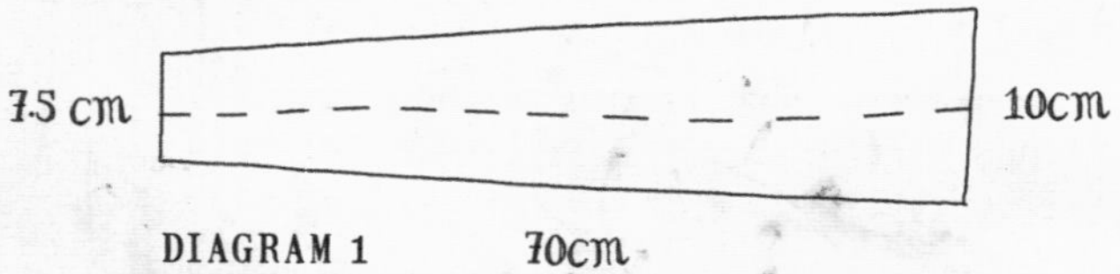

DIAGRAM 1

5. Fold the entire length of paper down the middle lengthways (this will be the snake's spine). Do not unfold this. Then, beginning at the wide end, start folding as if you were making a concertina. Start by making each fold 1cm wide, and gradually increase the folds until they are nearly 2cm wide. This gives the snake a nice structure.

6. Starting again at the wide end, fold the corners of the centre fold over into the valleys (see Diagram 2). This will give the snake's body a zigzag effect.

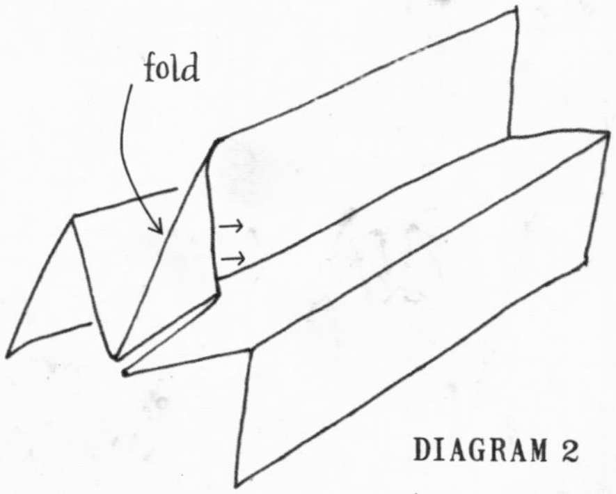

DIAGRAM 2

7. Once you've done all the folds, gently unravel the paper and spread it out. Refold it but this time one side of the snake folds upwards and the other side folds downwards as shown in the photo to the right. This takes a little patience and manipulation.

8. If the head is now completely dry, you can add the rubber band mechanism. First, either with a drill or metal skewer make 2 holes on either side of the snake's head. If you haven't already got 2 holes in a wooden cotton reel, or are using a wooden broom handle, drill them now. Thread the rubber band through the side holes of the snake's head and through the 2 holes of the cotton reel and tie off, tightly. You don't want any slack (see Diagram 3).

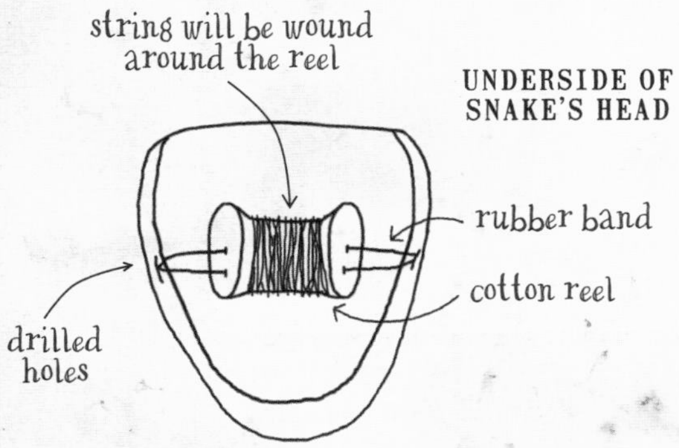

DIAGRAM 3

9. Using wallpaper paste, cover the snake's head with plain coloured or decorative paper. This will stop the rubber band from showing on the outside. Decorate the snake's head in any way you wish. Leave the head to dry.

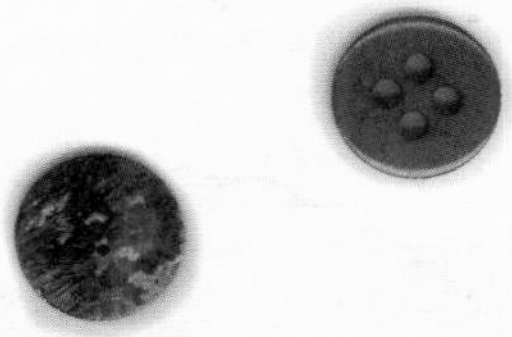

DIAGRAM 4

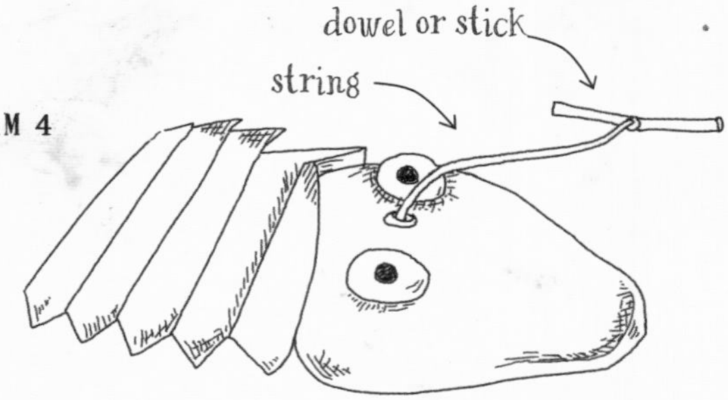

10 With the drill or skewer make a small hole in the centre of the snake's head above the cotton reel. Turn the cotton reel so the rubber band starts to wind up on either side of the reel. Hold the cotton reel firmly to stop the rubber band from twirling undone. Now, thread the length of string through the hole in the centre of the snake's head (you might need another pair of hands for this) and attach the end of the string to the cotton reel using a non-slip knot — remembering to keep the rubber band tightly wound. Attach the thin piece of dowel or stick at the other end of the string to make a handle (see Diagram 4). Now let go of the cotton reel and it should spin round and wind up the string. You now have a working rubber-band contraption!

11 Glue the wide end of the snake's body to the snake's head, using PVA glue. Let it dry.

12 Attach the buttons to the snake's head for the eyes, or, if you like, simply paint the eyes on.

13 Finally, pull the string so the cotton reel winds up, place your slinky snake on a smooth surface, release the pressure from the string and see your snake slither!

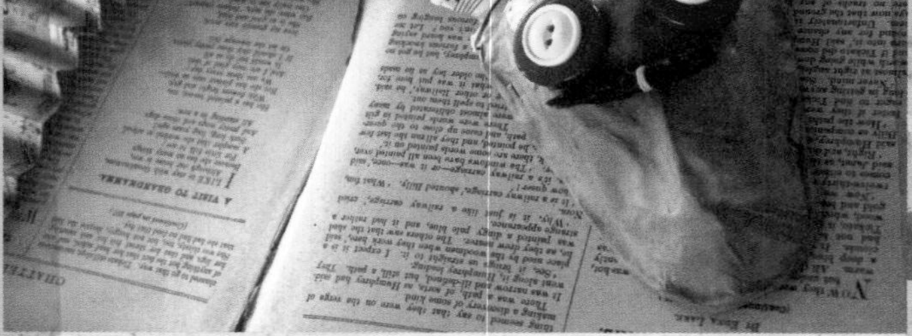

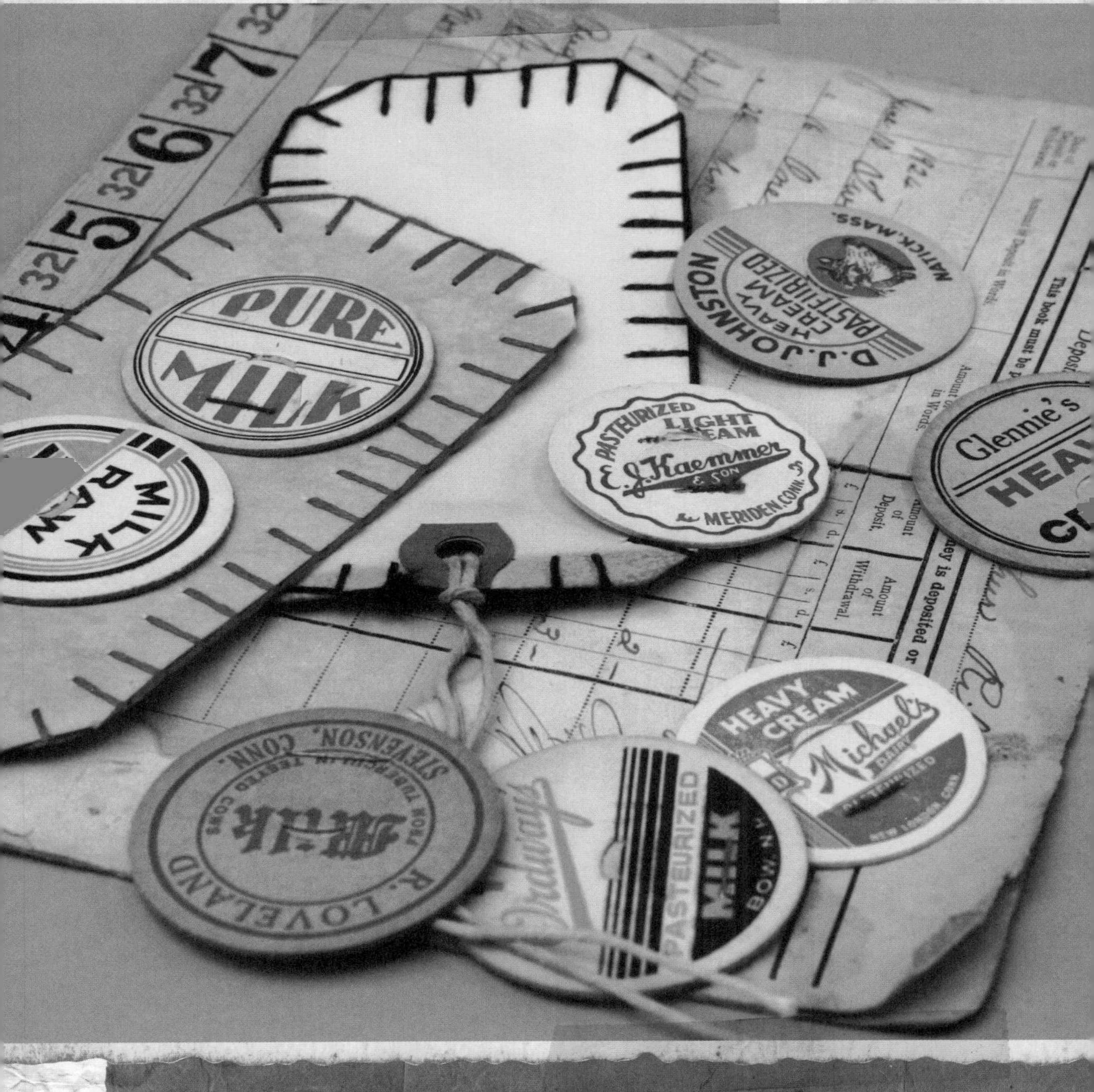

PURE
MILK
RAW
MILK
PASTEURIZED
LIGHT CREAM
J. Kaemmer
& SON
MERIDEN, CONN.
D. J. JOHNSTON
HEAVY
CREAM
PASTEURIZED
NATICK, MASS.
Glennie's
HEAVY
CREAM
Michael's
PASTEURIZED
MILK
R. LOVELAND
STEVENSON, CONN.
Milk

EASY

Accordion Card

This fold-out card is so lovely it really doubles as a gift. So save your pennies and make your fingers do the creating. Your friends will certainly appreciate this homemade effort.

YOU WILL NEED

Utility knife and cutting mat for adults or scissors for kids

Metal ruler

A3 sheet of 280gsm or heavier card, for end boards

2 single A4 sheets of 80gsm patterned paper

Spray adhesive

Brayer or rolling pin

2 x A3 sheet of 200–250gsm (cartridge-paper weight) white, textured paper for concertina or the long side of a piece of wrapping paper

Watercolour paints or rubber stamps

Contrasting strip of paper for outside, optional

String or ribbon, optional

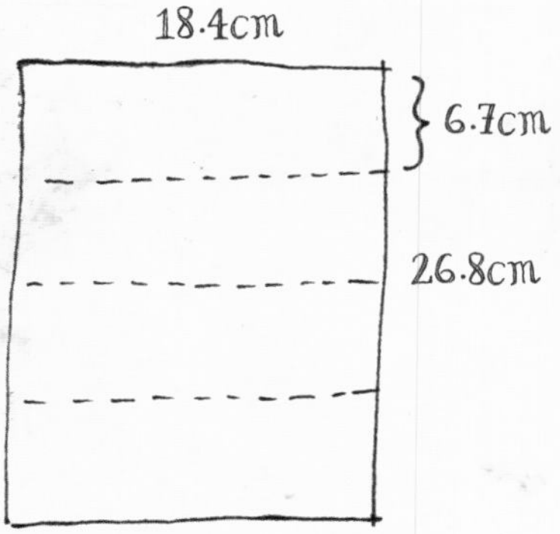

DIAGRAM 1

METHOD

1. Using the cutting mat, knife and metal ruler, cut out two identical end boards 19cm x 7cm from the 280gsm card to make the back and front of the accordion.

2. Cover the boards on both sides with your chosen patterned paper, using spray adhesive.* Choose the neatest sides for the front and back of the end boards. Don't worry too much about being neat on the insides as these will be covered with the white paper or wrap. Smooth any wrinkles and air bubbles with a brayer or rolling pin. Leave the end boards to dry.

3. While you're waiting for the end boards to dry, prepare your paper for folding. Decide how many pages you want. In Diagram 1, I've allowed for 4. Since you want the end boards to be slightly larger than the internal concertina, cut the white paper to 18.4cm x 26.8cm and score at 6.7cm intervals.

4. Paint or stamp your message onto your scored paper, with each letter falling evenly between each fold. Let the paint or stamps dry, then fold the scored lines concertina fashion. Check that it opens and closes properly.

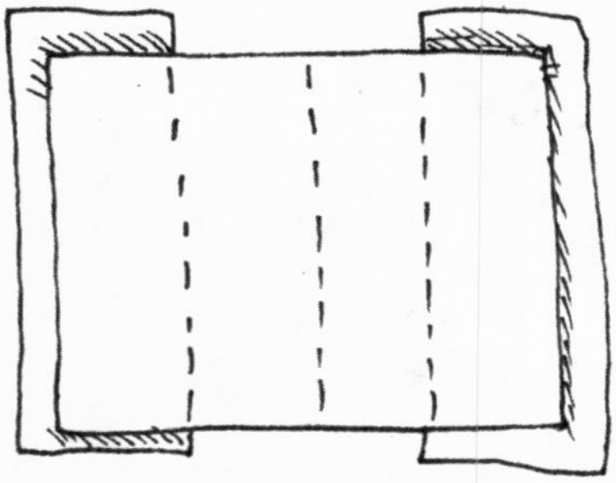

DIAGRAM 2

5. With spray adhesive, adhere the back (blank side) of the first concertina fold to the inside of the front end board, and then do the same with the back board (see Diagram 2).

6. Use a brayer or rolling pin to firmly sandwich the two together.

7. If you wish, glue a contrasting strip of paper to the outside of the card using spray adhesive. Take the paper slightly around the sides of the end boards so that it's neat. Cut a length of string or ribbon and tie a bow around your offering.

***NOTE Always use spray adhesive in a well-ventilated area — we do ours on a sheet of newspaper outside.**

IDEA

You can have great fun with these by extending the paper inside to make a much longer concertina. Personalise your card by adding tokens or motifs that relate to the receiver, or cut out odds and ends from newspapers and magazines and glue them to the outside.

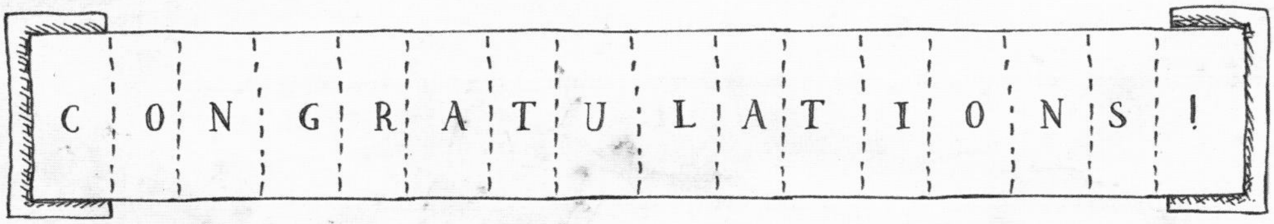

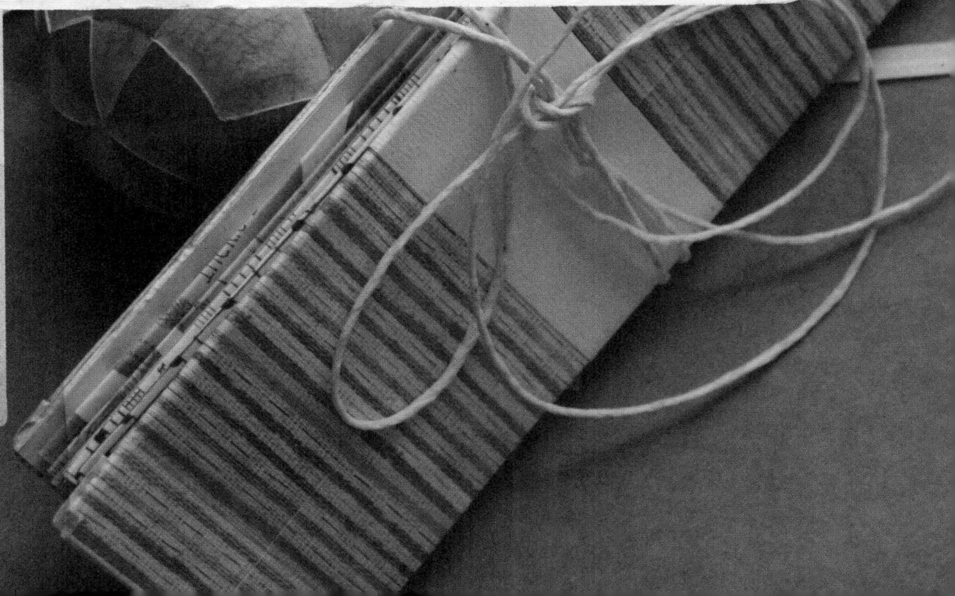

GREETINGS
POST CARD
TUCK'S POST CARD
97. Polygonaceae
Fagopyrum L.
Buchweizen.
POST CARD
FAVOURITE FLOWERS
The Address to be written on this side.
POST CARD
15cm角
10柄
10枚入
金剛
禪紙

eng

EASY

Twirling Hearts

This sweet little project came about from my experimenting with a heart-shaped hole punch that I picked up in a craft store. I punched dozens of hearts out of all kinds of paper and wondered what to do with them. After eschewing a design where all the different patterned hearts were lined up in rows, I realised that by folding them in half and fanning them out, I could make them into little ephemeral things that could also hang — rather like lanterns. A few stitches down the centre, ending at the top of the heart, allows them to twirl. They are quite delightful to watch when hanging in a window and caught by a breeze.

YOU WILL NEED

A variety of 'found' papers — thinner paper, about 90–100gsm is best as any thicker and the craft punch has trouble cutting it

A heart-shaped paper punch (mine was approximately 2.5cm across at its broadest) from a craft shop

Needle and thread

This is super easy.

1. Punch hearts from your papers …
2. Fold them in half vertically, so you have two halves of the heart.
3. Now flatten them again — you're effectively scoring them this way so that it's easier to find where you need to sew.
4. Stack about 6 hearts on top of each other.
5. Get your needle and thread (I doubled my thread over) and sew from one end of the crease to the other. Tie each piece of thread off with a knot.

IDEA

These are great scattered on a table as decorations or do a chain of them and make into a really pretty and unusual garland. Use old Christmas wrapping and bon-bon papers for a Christmassy look.

Resources

BOOKS AND MAGAZINES

The seminal books on freeing up your true artistic nature are Betty Edwards' *Drawing on the Right Side of the Brain* (Souvenir Press, London, 1981) and Julia Cameron's *The Artist's Way* (Putnam, New York, 2002).

Many other good books have been written along these lines as well, including Natalie Goldberg's *Living Color – A Writer Paints Her World* (Bantam, New York, 1997). A lovely more recent title is Lynda Barry's, *Picture This: The Near-sighted Monkey Book* (Drawn and Quarterly, US, 2010). I just love how this author embraces and utilises mess. Also see her book *What It Is* (Drawn and Quarterly Publishers, Canada, 2011), which is ostensibly about writing but covers the creative spectrum.

Other books that are full of ideas, include: *Creating Sketchbooks for Embroiderers and Textile Artists* by Kay Greenlees (Batsford, UK, 2005). Even though this book is primarily aimed at textile artists, it is a rich resource for the paper-and-art lover.

A wonderful inspiration and resource is *The Book as Art: Artists' Books from the National Museum of Women in the Arts* by Krystyna Wasserman (Princeton Architectural Press, New York, 2007). It includes some great ideas for making and keeping sketchbooks of your work and it includes some projects by the very clever Audrey Niffenegger. Wonderful paper engineering possibilities are scattered throughout.

Lisa Occhipinti's book *The Repurposed Library* (Stewart, Tabori and Chang, New York, 2011) is a paean to the art of making something new out of humble books.

UPPERCASE Magazine is a great resource for crafty types. Beautifully designed and full of inspirational people and projects.

Paper Runway is an Australian-based quarterly magazine for paper lovers. **www.paperrunway.com.**

Individual Artists and Inspiring Sites

AUDREY NIFFENEGGER
is a very talented writer and artist who thinks outside the square.
www.audreyniffenegger.com

MARY EMMA HAWTHORNE
does amazing paper collages that I just love. See especially the birds and boxes section.
www.maryemmahawthorne.com

CYBELE YOUNG
is a Canadian artist who does the most amazing tiny sculptures from Japanese paper. See her section on sculpture.
www.cybeleyoung.ca

PETER CALLESEN
is an artist who makes a lot of his work out of A4 sheets of paper. His paper castle and church interiors are fascinating.
www.petercallesen.com

JOLIS PAONS
uses newspapers and phone books to make some pretty convincing paper couture.
www.flickr.com/photos/jolispaons/sets/72157604766091529

BERT SIMONS
creates life-like portraits of people from tiny pieces of paper, printed with photographic details, which are then cut out and glued together.
www.bertsimons.nl/portfolio/papersculptures

CHRIS KENNY
a UK based artist, is very talented and often uses maps and bits of text in his works. Finely cut, painstakingly detailed hanging on a pin head.
www.englandgallery.com

There is a movement among those who make art from existing books that is called 'altered books'. I really admire this craft as it uses a most humble object to create quite breathtakingly beautiful artworks. The 'altered book' project in this book is very simple, but the following folks below know a thing or two about complicating their pastime with lots of tiny cutting of the whole book.

SU BLACKWELL
sculpts amazing scenes from books. See her Wildflowers, 2007, and Woodcutters Hut, 2008, in the portfolio of her work on her site.
www.sublackwell.co.uk

BRIAN DETTMER
brings in illustration and text to his labyrinthine, almost mechanical-looking paper sculptures.
www.briandettmer.com

YUKEN TERUYA
uses old Burger King and McDonalds wrappers to make amazing little landscapes and images.
www.saatchi-gallery.co.uk/artists/yuken_teruya_biography

CHRISSIE MACDONALD
a UK artist, does some very crafty things with bold, simple paper pieces.
www.chrissiemacdonald.co.uk

JULENE HARRISON
does some extraordinary filigree-like paper cutting.
www.madebyjulene.com

BENJA HARNEY
(Paperform) creates formal paper sculptures of everyday objects, infusing them with calm and beauty.
www.paperform.wordpress.com

LUCILLE MORONI
includes stitching in her finely crafted works. Lucilles work can be found on tumblr and elle decoration blog.

NORIKO AMBE
is an interesting conceptual paper artist.
www.norikoambe.com

REBECCA J COLES
makes lovely paper sculptures.
www.rebeccajcoles.co.uk

PETER CLARK
is one of my faves … what a talent, from the UK, he uses found papers in his amazing collages.
www.peterclarkcollage.com

ANNA-WILI HIGHFIELD
is an amazingly talented young Sydney woman who fashions sculpture out of humble old paper.
www.annawilihighfield.com

SHERIDAN JONES
is a Melbourne based artist who does some amazing stuff with paper to make beautiful sculptures.
www.thelaundryroompressandstudio.blogspot.com

AYAME KIKUCHI
is a Japanese artist who has the most wonderful range of paper bird cards I've ever seen. I found her on the website Pinterest.
www.pinterest.com/pin/26732238

CLARE GODDARD
makes artworks from vintage papers and found objects which are just lovely.
www.claregoddard.com

MAGIE HOLLINGWORTH
makes some pretty appealing stuff out of papier-mâché. I love the garden tools especially.
www.magiehollingworth.co.uk

GRACIA HABY AND LOUISE JENNISON
make divine limited edition artists' books and zines.
www.gracialouise.com

BERDIEN NIEUWENHUIZEN
wonderful wall hangings and sculptures.
www.berdien-nieuwenhuizen.kunstinzicht.nl

PAPER CUT PROJECT
makes amazing paper couture.
www.paper-cut-project.com

THE SKETCHBOOK PROJECT
is a lovely US initiative that collects artists' sketchbooks and exhibits them annually. There is some lovely work on paper here.
www.arthousecoop.com

PINTEREST
is a great site to see a real collection of exciting new work, including that by paper artistes.
www.pinterest.com

Purchasing Supplies

My favourite paper and card-lovers shops are, perhaps unsurprisingly, in Sydney, as they're the ones I frequent the most. But here is a list that includes paper suppliers in other Australian states as well:

For general art and craft supplies look up your closest art supply shop as well as you nearest Lincraft, Spotlight and Hobbyco stores. Eckersleys is also good.

New South Wales

AMAZING PAPER
184 Enmore Road
Enmore NSW 2042
(02)9519 8237

PULP CREATIVE PAPER
294 Sydney Road
Balgowlah NSW 2093
(02) 9948 1191

PAPIER D'AMOUR
4 Cross Street
Double Bay NSW 2028
(02) 9362 5200

PAPER 2
477 Crown Street
Surry Hills
(02) 9318 1121

OXFORD ART SUPPLIES & BOOKS
Victoria Avenue
Chatswood, NSW 206
(02) 9417 8572
and
221-225 Oxford Street
Darlinghurst NSW 2010
(02) 9360 4066

NEWSPAPER TAXI
247 Australia St
Newtown NSW 2042
0421 981 182

LITTLE PAPER LANE
5/1751 Pittwater Road
Mona Vale NSW 2103
(02) 8407 9204

KINOKUNYA
500 George Street
Sydney NSW 2000
(02) 9262 7996

PAPER EMPORIUM
438 Dean Street
Albury NSW 2640
(02) 6021 6211

LITTLE PAPERCUP
Shop 18/19
Market Square
Hunter Street Mall
Newastle

Victoria

CLASSY PAPIERE
206 Camberwell Road
Hawthorn East Vic 3149
(03) 9813 2600

HANDWORKS
244 Chapel Street
Prahran Vic 3181
(03) 9533 8566

PAPER CACHE
566 Main Street
Mordialloc Vic 3195
(03) 9587 8899

ROCK PAPER SCISSORS
1266 High Street
Armadale Vic 3143
(03) 9500 1335

CARD AND CABOODLE
3 stores in Melbourne:

TG18 Goldsbrough Lane
550 Bourke Street
Melbourne Vic 3000
(03) 9600 0621

The Block Arcade
Shop 18 & 19
98-100 Elizabeth St
Melbourne Vic 3000
(03) 9650 9011

Chadstone Shopping Centre
Shop B 136A
Chadstone Shopping Centre
Chadstone Vic 3148
(03) 9568 1199

Queensland

CARD AND CABOODLE
Queens Plaza Shop LG02A
226 Queen Street
Brisbane Qld 4000
(07) 3229 3800

MONOGRAMS FINE PAPERS
Shop 4, Savoir Faire
20 Park Road,
Milton Qld 4064

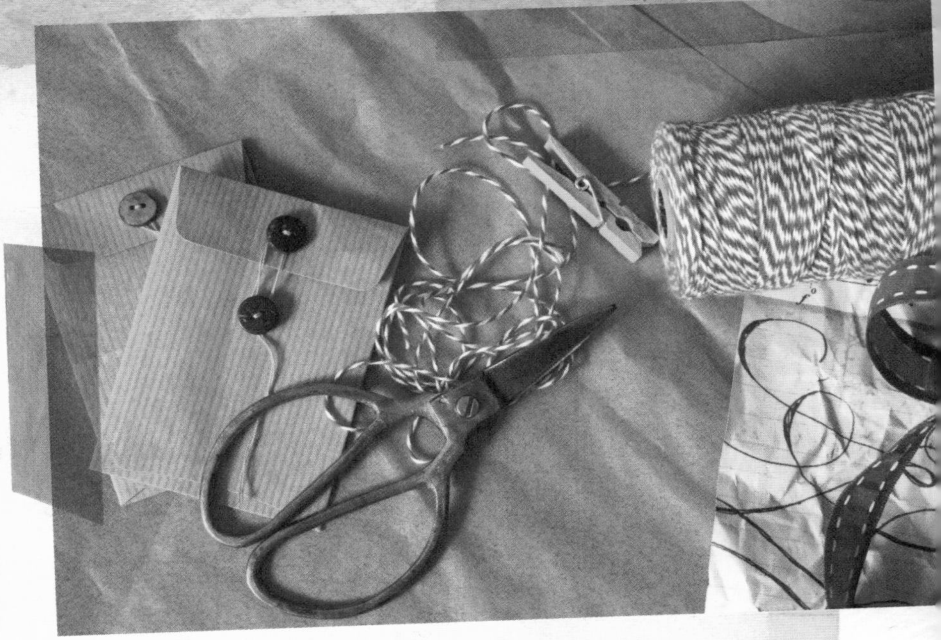

A CRAFT AFFAIR STATIONERY AND INVITATIONS
Cnr Anne & Casey Sts
Aitkenvale (Townsville)
Qld 4814
(07) 4728 2044

THE PAPER CONNECTION
201 Charlotte Street
Brisbane Qld 4000
(07) 3229 3088

CRACKER PRINT & PAPER
Harrison House
435 Ruthven Street
Toowoomba QLD 4350
(07) 4632 3522

South Australia

COLIN MURCH OFFICE EQUIPMENT
41-43 Kensington Road
Norwood SA 5071
(08) 8332 5569

Northern Territory

CHIGGY'S PLACE
PO Box 1222
Palmerston NT 830
(08) 8931 1360

Tasmania

CREATIVE PAPER TASMANIA
2 Bass Highway
(Western side of Burnie CBD on highway)
Po Box 973
Burnie Tasmania
(03) 6430 5831

Western Australia

ANNIE P. PAPERIE
243 Stirling Highway
Claremont WA 6010
(8) 9384 6035

Shopping online

Though I ardently implore you to use what you have around you, I do occasionally tempt myself with looking through online sites for something different.

For interesting old papers for collage and bits of ephemera I go to the ever-loveable ETSY site. **www.etsy.com** Do a search through collage, vintage and/or found papers, you will be amazed what turns up.

Also for a cool little site with all things designy in the paper goods area, look at **www.feltandwireshop.com**

For Skye's card and stationery designs see:

www.skyesthelimit.com.au

Skye also licenses her artwork to other companies. So if you see something suspiciously 'Skye' it probably is hers.

lesung aus
it als Dozent.
er schon fest.
uß der Akt
. Und ein

love xxx

PUBLIC SCHOOL SAVINGS

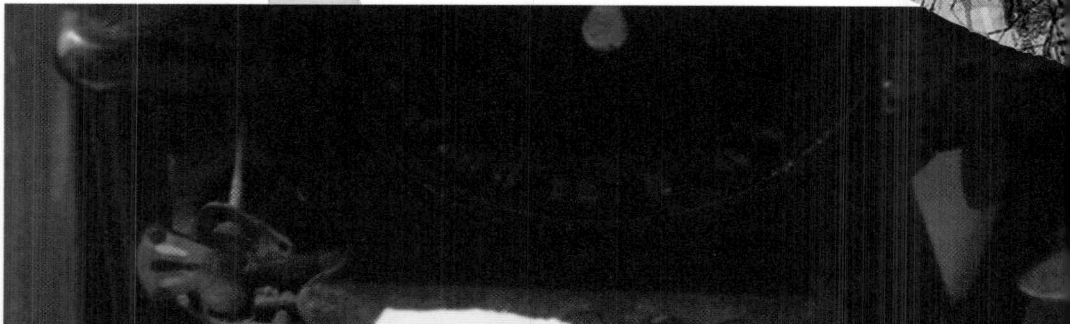
thankyou

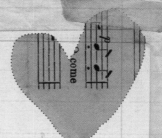

Thanks & Acknowledgements

With big heartfelt thanks to many helpers along the way: Badger and boys, Richmond, Captain Mikey (for his extreme perseverance with binding books), Margaret Leahy, Justy, Mim and Lek, Andy for top tips, Natalie Hudson and Chris Chun for feedback. My Mum and Dad who still can't believe their crazy artist daughter has found a way to feed herself.

Jenny and the girls from the 'Tron', who don't yet quite realise how clever they really are. With thanks to Jenny for the wonderful idea of crepe paper coasters. Who else would dream them up?

Thanks to Annie Aitken for the beautiful bag/vessel photographed with 'Articulated Girl' on page 157. Annie is both a good friend and wonderfully creative artist who sometimes dabbles in paper, www.annieaitken.com.

To the Gong gang — a great team of very able people who help keep the wheels turning at Skye's the Limit HQ, especially Jan, Glen, Fiona and Kim.

And thanks, as always to Margaret Connolly, my steady, patient and enthusiastic agent.

With thanks also to online resources that help me create some lovely works at times: www.fuzzimo.com and graphics fairy: www.graphicsfairy.blogspot.com

Also, if you want to make your own font like I did go to: www.yourfonts.com

At Harper Collins many thanks go to Roz Hopkins, who was always enthusiastic about my dream for this book. Julia Collingwood, who, as my editor, endured many hours and days making good my sometimes nonsensical projects. Many thanks to another 'Tron' gal, designer Natalie Winter, who steered her way through all kinds of preciousness and preening from me to arrive at a very pleasing look for *Paper Bliss.* Thank you.

HarperCollins*Publishers*

First published in Australia in 2012
by HarperCollins*Publishers* Australia Pty Limited
ABN 36 009 913 517
harpercollins.com.au

HarperCollins*Publishers*
Level 13, 201 Elizabeth Street, Sydney NSW 2000, Australia
31 View Road, Glenfield, Auckland 0627, New Zealand
A 53, Sector 57, Noida, UP, India
77–85 Fulham Palace Road, London W6 8JB, United Kingdom
2 Bloor Street East, 20th floor, Toronto, Ontario M4W 1A8, Canada
10 East 53rd Street, New York NY 10022, USA

National Library of Australia Cataloguing-in-Publication entry:
Rogers, Skye
Paper bliss / Skye Rogers.
ISBN: 9780732293444 (hbk.)
Paper work
Cut-out craft.
Paper art.

736.98

Cover and internal design by Natalie Winter
Cover and internal photographs by Skye Rogers
All decorative paper designed by skyes the limit
Typeset in Charter by Natalie Winter
Colour reproduction by Graphic Print Group, Adelaide
Printed and bound in China by RR Donnelley on 140gsm Lucky Bird Woodfree

5 4 3 2 1 11 12 13 14